"WHY"

A young girl's search for the truth

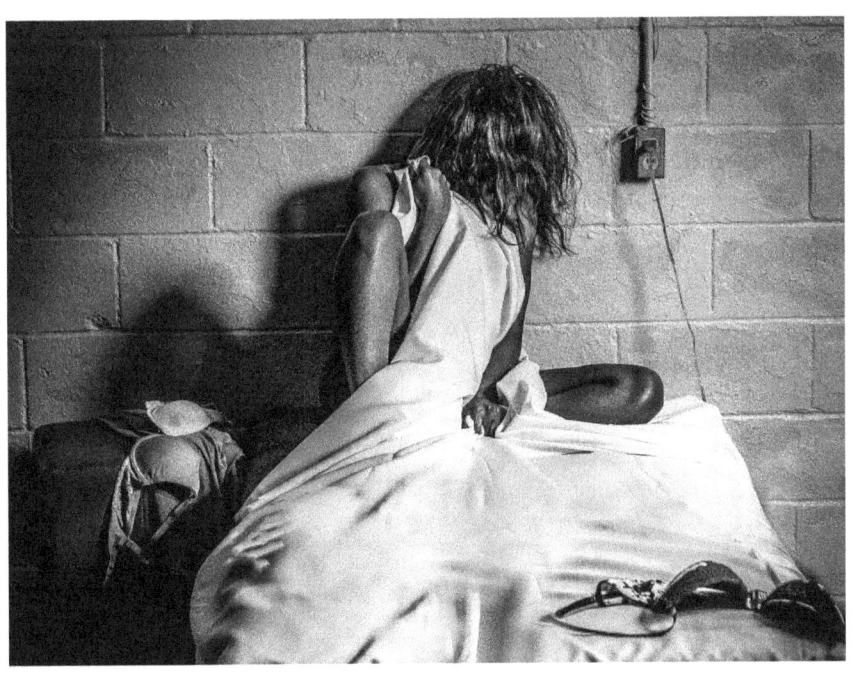

A Novel
by
Lakina Fulks

By Lakina Fulks
© 2018 Lakina Fulks
Printed in the United States of America
ISBN 978-0-578210-55-1

All rights reserved solely by the author. The author guarantees all contents are original and do not infringe upon the legal rights of any other person or work. No part of this book may be reproduced, stored in a retrieval system, or transmitted in any form or by any means without expressed written permission of the author.

Scriptures marked NKJV are taken from The Holy Bible, King James Version. Copyright © 1972 by Thomas Nelson Inc., Camden, New Jersey 08103.

Contact the author at lakinatheauthor@gmail.com
www.lakinatheauthor.com

Editor: Kori Winters
Photographer For Book Cover Sophia Gilmore
Book Cover Model Keturah Tolbert
Printed in the U.S.A.

DEDICATION

THIS BOOK IS dedicated to my beloved, late Apostle Hattie Patterson. She was not only a mentor but my spiritual mother. She pushed me to write this book. She told me God needed me to write this book to help set women free. After she told me that, I finally decided to do what God told me to do. It took four long arduous years, but I did it!! This book is also dedicated to my six children. No matter what challenges life brings your way, if you don't give up, you can come through it and it will make you stronger.

I also dedicate this book to my readers; the people that wanted to give up but couldn't and didn't. To those who vowed not to quit on themselves no matter how hard life got. Believe and know that you are destined for greatness and you have a purpose and a calling on your life!

FOREWORD

WHEN READING THIS book you will start a journey of both being enlighten and transformation. The graphic description of pain that Trinity has suffered will leave the reader reconsidering their own circumstances and decisions that are before them. When faced with a dysfunctional upbringing the first thing one must find is the courage to make decisions that breed healing. As a Pastor, I have counseled many people who do not have the courage to follow the path of healing. Therefore, they remain in dysfunctional and toxic circumstances and are held back from becoming what God had ordained for them to be. Many people who go through life under the pressure that is described in this book never find a place of wholeness. Besides being bound by suppressive memories they are also haunted by burning questions of why they are going through all of this. It is with this mindset the enemy infiltrates the thinking of the individual who has had to bear these types of circumstances. The enemy will whisper things like God as abandoned you or He does not love you. These are lies and even though things get tough the truth is God can still work His will in from any circumstance we face. This book will give courage to those who are in desperate need of wholeness and truth. My heart is that the reader will experience the necessary truth to set them free.

Pastor Gayle Brannan

PREFACE

There has been people telling me that I need to write a book. Someone even approached me after church meeting, telling me I needed to write a book about my life. That was right after I left my first husband. I was going to call it "Men Who Beat Their Wives." But I quickly realized that marriage was not going to be happily ever after, but yet another failed marriage. Through my second divorce and separation, the Lord began healing me and speaking to me about a book. But it wasn't until my dear Apostle asked me if I had seriously put forth the effort again. She knew it was from God, especially since I had been speaking to me about writing the book. I knew I had the book prepared.

It was a fall day when I had met with a friend to talk about the book. She said I needed a title, but all I kept thinking on was getting the book started. Later that night, the Lord spoke and said the title of my book would be called "Why." I asked why that title and He just kept repeating "Why?" As I began to ponder on this I realized that in all of my hardships, I've always asked the Lord, why? Why are all these bad things happening to me? There were so many whys in my past, but it was not until I finished this book that my whys were finally answered.

Lakina Fulks
July 4, 2018

Lakina Fulks

ACKNOWLEDGMENTS

I WOULD LIKE to thank my friend, my go-to person, an awesome woman of God, Debra Watkins-Flowers. Without her, I don't know how this book would have come together. She labored with me long nights on this book. She had the same vision for this book as I did. She was truly sent by God to help me write this book. I am forever grateful for her diligence, prayers, and commitment. She has been such a blessing. It's so awesome when God places a person in your life to see your vision, and to hear it and to believe it. It's truly something to cherish.

To my children, who were there for me since day one, listening to every chapter, not criticizing me, not judging me, but always supporting me. Sometimes they would cry saying, "Mom we didn't know all that stuff happened to you!" My children rock! They are truly my gifts from God.

And last, but definitely not least, to my dear husband, my Prince Charming, my true happily ever after. Thank you for your understanding, love, support and openness to me. It was after I met you that I knew it was time to finish my book. I knew it was time to close those old chapters and write new ones with you.

Lakina Fulks

INTRODUCTION

THIS BOOK WILL captivate you. It will make you feel things you've never felt before. This book is raw and honest. It is not for the faint of heart. It will soothe your spirit and make you angry all in one sentence. You will get to know the characters intimately. Their lives and who they are will jump off of the pages at you! You will be able to see yourself in some of these characters or you'll know someone just like them. This book will deliver you, and it may even haunt you because of your own past. But rest assured, it will teach you to love and have empathy for others on a greater level.

From a young girl to a middle-aged woman, you will journey through the life of Trinity. You will experience her joys and her many pains. You will witness her abuse and come to know her abusers. You will become so invested in Trinity that you will not be able to put this book down. In the end, you will have laughed, cried, yelled and asked the question "why" several times. No one comes out of reading this book without being changed. **"WHY"** is a necessary book about change and deliverance. It will keep you on the edge of your seat until the final page is read. It is an all-too-familiar story that ends in truth. **"WHY"** is not only a book to be read but a book to be experienced!

TABLE OF CONTENTS

Dedication iii
Foreword iv
Preface v
Acknowledgments vi
Introduction vii

1. Stolen Innocence 1
2. God Uses the Broken Ones 5
3. Cousin Paul 7
4. Fairytale Husband 9
5. My Sister's Keeper 21
6. Trinity's Best Friend 23
7. Red's Girl 33
8. Granny 37
9. First Lady by Day, Prostitute by Night 41
10. Dope House Dancer 45
11. Trinity Meets the Husband She Prayed For 49
12. The Producer 55
13. Having the Courage to Leave 59
14. The Devil Tried to Trick Trinity 65
15. I Was His Personal Savior and Drug Mule 71
16. Dating the Old Fashioned Way 81
17. Trinity's Broken Baby 85
18. The Wedding Day 93
19. Elder Mitchell's Story is Still Being Written 99
20. WHY 103

About the Author 107

CHAPTER 1

(Stolen Innocence)

TRINITY RAN UPSTAIRS and locked the bathroom door. She was so scared and so tired of it all. *Why won't anyone help me?* She kept thinking. The footsteps drew closer to the bathroom door and just as Trinity looked up to see the knob turning, her mother called her downstairs for dinner. "Whew!" Trinity exclaimed. For now, she was safe.

Trinity had always been a "special child." She was different than the other children. She never played like the other children and she never danced liked the other little girls. For a time, Trinity felt something was wrong with her, but she always heard this little voice that kept telling her "you are special." She had four sisters and one brother. Trinity was the oldest. She always felt she had to protect her youngest sister Tasha. Besides, Trinity liked being bossy. Everyone said Trinity was like her mother, but Trinity didn't think so. She always felt she was more like her dad. She was a daddy's girl.

Trinity went to church, read her bible and at an early age, began praying and establishing a relationship with God. She came from a middle-class family who was the envy of the neighborhood and the church. Her mother doted on the idea of a perfect family, but things were not so perfect for Trinity. Trinity's family was very religious; her mother raised her as a good Christian girl. Trinity couldn't wear pants to church, only dresses. She was a young girl, but unbeknownst to her family, she was engaging in adult activity. Her only confidant was her younger brother Henry. Henry knew all of Trinity's secrets.

As Trinity ran downstairs to eat dinner with her family, her brother and his friends came home and rushed upstairs. Trinity wondered what

(Stolen Innocence)

was so important that they didn't stop to get something to eat. *When do boys pass up food?* She thought. Her mother snapped Trinity out of thought by telling her to put on her white dress to wear to bible study tonight. "Why do I have to wear that dress to bible study? Can I wear something else?" Trinity asked.

"No," her mother answered. "You look so cute in your white dress, like a perfect little princess." Even though Trinity was only nine years old, she didn't feel like a perfect little princess. She felt alone and dirty; too dirty to wear that white dress. But it didn't matter how she felt because in her mother's eyes she was perfect. Trinity was considered the pretty one of her sisters. Not only did she have to fend off the boys, but sometimes her sisters were jealous of her. She always felt like she had to do extra to be genuinely liked or loved.

Church was especially long tonight, but Trinity didn't mind because she loved going to church. It was the only place she felt safe. She knew if no one else could save her, love her or even protect her, God would. But lately, she kept asking God, *"why?" "Why didn't you protect me?"* Trinity trusted what church meant and she trusted the people in the church. She trusted her bible, she trusted the Word of God and she even trusted the men in the church, but that trust would soon be tested as well. Trinity came home from church and rushed to go to bed so she could fantasize about a normal life; a husband and being happy. Instead, Trinity began to remember an incident that happened during the summer.

Trinity and her family were going to a picnic. She was excited because for one day she didn't have to worry about her older cousin Paul.

"Everybody, let's go get in the car," Trinity's father yelled. They were on their way to the family picnic. Trinity loved going to the park because it was the only place where she could play and feel like a little girl without having to worry about someone bothering her.

"I'm sitting by the window," yelled Henry.

Henry always wanted the window seat and Tasha always sat in the middle. These were good memories, when the whole family was together and everybody was happy.

"Y'all better use the bathroom before we leave," said Trinity's mother.

"WHY"

Her brother and sisters jumped out of the car to go use the bathroom, but Trinity stayed. She didn't have to go and didn't want anything to slow them down from getting to the park. There was a swing set with her name on it and she couldn't wait to get there!

The air was filled with the smell of barbeque. Hot dogs and hamburgers were on the grill and the Isley Brothers were playing in the background. The adults were laughing and talking loud while Trinity's sisters, brother and cousins were having a ball. The sun felt so good on Trinity's face. Today was a good day, she thought.

"Hey Sissy, come and push me!" Tasha yelled at Trinity. Sissy was Trinity's nickname. Trinity ran over to push Tasha on the swing. They laughed and giggled and then reality came back to slap Trinity in the face when Tasha said, "I don't want to go back home, Sissy. What if it happens again tonight?"

"I won't let anything happen to you, Tasha. Just have fun and don't think about it," Trinity responded. But Trinity knew she was lying to her little sister. How could she help her if she couldn't help herself?

"Mom, I have to go the bathroom," Trinity said to her mother. But her mother was having too much fun, so she told Trinity to ask her cousin Paul to take her. Trinity's eyes got so big that her mother asked her what was wrong. Trinity couldn't answer — she just stood there in shock. *Did my mother just tell me to ask Paul to take me to the bathroom? She must be out of her mind*, Trinity thought.

> "Well, don't just stand there, speak up. What's wrong with you?" said Trinity's mother. "Nothing is wrong mom, I just wanted you to take me that's all," said Trinity.
>
> "Well I'm cooking right now, so just go and ask your cousin Paul to take you."

Trinity was in the bathroom for such a long time that her father asked her, "what did you have to do, a Number Two?"

Trinity just looked at her father, speechless. She wanted to cry, but she dared not say a word. Her father looked at her as if he knew something was wrong, but he never said anything. *No one ever says anything in this family*, Trinity thought. She wanted to tell her mother but who

(Stolen Innocence)

would believe her? The last thing Trinity wanted to do was make everybody upset. So she did what she knew how to do, which was keep her mouth shut.

Trinity didn't remember much of what happened in the bathroom, but she did remember walking funny when she came out, and Paul telling her not to tell anyone. As Trinity lay in the bed remembering that day, she believed that was the first time God turned His back on her. Her parents didn't protect her, her brother and sisters couldn't protect her, so only God was left and He turned His back on her too. That was the day Trinity began to feel alone and dirty.

The next morning, Trinity was awakened by the smell of pancakes.

"Y'all, come and get your breakfast," yelled Trinity's mother. Trinity didn't really want to eat. She just wanted to go to school. Trinity liked school because she got good grades. It had always been a place that made Trinity feel good about herself, and no one could take that away from her. These good grades were hers and hers alone. Good grades made Trinity feel proud and strong. Even at a young age, she figured that if she could keep good grades while going through all the bad stuff at home, then she had to be strong.

Little did Trinity know, someday her strength and her good grades would help mold her into a disciplined young woman. Trinity would go through hell in her life, but she would never let anyone take away her education. That was hers and no one could have it.

CHAPTER 2

(God Uses the Broken Ones)

Ephesians 5:27 New King James Version (NKJV)

[27] that He might present her to Himself a glorious church, not having spot or wrinkle or any such thing, but that she should be holy and without blemish.

GOD IS ABLE to cleanse us, wash us, heal us and prepare us to do service for His kingdom. Trinity had begun her journey of healing when she took control over her life in a manner that would be pleasing to God. Grace, Trinity's grandmother had taught her years ago how to enter into God's presence and when all else failed, Trinity prayed — that's one thing she knew how to do. Trinity's former years had been filled and soiled with sin. Some sin was brought on by Trinity and some was not. Some sin came about from Trinity just trying to survive — too many people were counting on her. She didn't know it at the time, but God would eventually send people to her so she could share her story and help heal others as God was healing her. With transition comes inner strength.

Trinity was no punk when it came to prayer. She knew she had gifts and that there would come a time when God would begin guiding her in those gifts. Trinity knew that God would use her testimony one day, but she was scared and apprehensive about people knowing her business — especially her parents. She couldn't speak about things in her family. Her mother would hate her for that. But Trinity remembered that all through the Bible, God used people who were flawed. He used

(God Uses the Broken Ones)

Elijah to oppose a wicked king and to restore the land despite him being suicidal and suffering from depression. God also used Gideon to free the people of Israel and condemn their idolatry despite Gideon being afraid. God used Rahab, a prostitute, to help the Israelites capture the city of Jericho. He used David who was an adulterer and a murderer but made him king. Trinity knew that God used countless flawed people throughout the Bible, but she still didn't feel comfortable about telling her own story.

God uses people who have a heart and that trust Him and now God was beginning to call on Trinity to trust Him with the telling of her testimony. That would be a hard thing for Trinity to do, especially in church. Only her sisters and brother knew some of the things that went on in their house when they were kids. Now she was being asked to tell about it in church.

"Are you really going to tell everybody about the stuff we went through?" Tasha asked.

"Yeah, I have to," Trinity said. "I've held these secrets too long and I'm tired of walking in fear."

How many of you know that fear paralyzes us from being great, and doing great things? Fear takes away all of our power and zest for life. Fear controls our decision-making and pulls us further away from God. When God begins to use us, He will use that very thing that we are afraid of to set us free. When we are no longer able to hide from our fears, we begin to live in truth and are not hindered by what other people think. Our only concern should be pleasing the Lord. Being set free from our fears is a matter of life and death, and Trinity had been dead for so long that it had become the norm. However, all of that was about to change when Trinity began visiting Apostle Love's church. It would be there that she would begin to experience love that she had never known before — from God and from man.

But she had to go through hell first.

CHAPTER 3

(Cousin Paul)

"GET IN THE damn closet!" Trinity's cousin Paul shouted. She had become used to this. If only her mother knew what her cousin Paul was making her and her sister do.

"Nah man, I don't wanna do it," said Paul's friend.

"Go head man," said Paul, "She'll let you do it." Paul had told his friend to put his penis in Tasha's mouth, but his friend didn't want to do it because Tasha was so young,

"Watch this," said Paul. Trinity knew she had to think fast. She didn't want her sister Tasha to do it, so instead of making Tasha do it, Trinity volunteered. Paul didn't care who did it; he just wanted it done.

After Paul finished, Trinity pulled the hair out of her mouth that had gotten stuck in between her teeth.

"Come on Tasha, let's go," Trinity said.

Strangely, Trinity felt relieved because Paul didn't touch her younger sister. Paul was sixteen years old when it all started. Trinity and Tasha were only eight and nine years old, and even back then Trinity always felt like she was the protector. But when was someone going to protect her?

Henry, Trinity's younger brother, always had friends over.

"Hey, Henry, where is your sister? Henry's friend asked.

Henry's friends liked going over Henry's house for more reasons than just playing with him. Trinity was popular with Henry's friends because Trinity would do things to Henry's friends that had been done to her. Henry and his friends were about nine or ten years old at the time, and Trinity was between the ages of twelve and fourteen when

(Cousin Paul)

she began molesting her younger brother's friends. Even though Trinity didn't like what was being done to her, she sexually abused Henry's friends. She didn't understand it, but she had an urge that needed to be fed.

Some nights, Trinity and Tasha would lie in the bed with intense pain between their legs. It was so bad that they taught themselves "a squeezing technique." They would put a pillow between their legs and squeeze so the pain and the sexual desire would go away.

Is something wrong with me? Am I a bad person? Trinity thought. She loved God and she had faith in God, but surely this was not of God. Why? Why? Why was this happening to her? Sometimes Trinity couldn't always save Tasha, and Tasha began to be abused by Paul as well.

"Why can't we tell mom?" Tasha asked. "Why can't we tell somebody? I'm tired of this and I'm tired of being sore." Trinity tried to calm her sister down before someone heard her. She didn't know how to answer Tasha's questions because she always felt that no one would believe her. She didn't want to upset anybody, and she didn't want anyone to know how dirty she felt. She didn't know it then, but Trinity was teaching her sister to become silent as well. Both sisters would soon grow up to accept abuse silently.

It's funny how things work out. For a long time, Paul had Trinity and Tasha in a silent hell, chained to an emotional prison, unable to speak, their voices silenced. Now years later, that same man who put them in a physical and emotional prison was now in a prison of his own. One night Paul went to a party and somebody put something in his drink and he never was the same after that. He started using drugs and even attempted to kill himself. Once, the police caught him talking to a telephone pole. Soon after that, he was admitted to a mental institution. Even though Paul couldn't hurt Trinity or her sister ever again, he hurt their souls — and that pain was pain only God could fix.

CHAPTER 4

(Fairytale Husband)

"SHUT YOUR ASS up with all that crying!" Derek yelled. He had no concern for the pain that he had caused, nor did he think he had done anything wrong. The apologies were never enough because he would continue to hit, punch, scream and call Trinity names until all she knew how to do was survive. She had traded one type of hell for another. She got pregnant at sixteen and married Derek at seventeen. Trinity only married him because she wanted to get out; out of her mother's house, out of the streets and out of the beds that held her in bondage. Even though now she was in this beautiful home, she was still in physical and emotional pain. As Trinity lay in the bed, bleeding because Derek split her lip, she kept thinking, *Why, Lord? Why is this happening to me? He is supposed to love me.* Trinity was talking about her husband Derek, who showed his affection — or lack thereof — with his fists.

Trinity met Derek when she was fifteen. He used to chase her around the church. Trinity thought, *this man must be crazy to chase me around the church,* but there was something about him that Trinity liked. Derek liked Trinity as well. One evening after Bible study, Derek asked one of Trinity's friends for her telephone number, but they never hooked up until Trinity was sixteen. Trinity knew Derek was older than her but she didn't care. She was drawn to Derek not just because of his looks, his cars and his clothes, but his ministry as well. Trinity had already run away from her parents' house a few times before she met Derek, so when they began seeing each other, Trinity wanted to be with Derek all of the time. Derek spoiled Trinity and she loved it. Derek had Trinity driving around in a BMW at sixteen. Trinity's parents

(Fairytale Husband)

thought he was the perfect man for her but as usual, they didn't know Trinity's truths and they had no idea who Derek really was. Trinity never got to know Derek either. He had told her he was much younger, and that lie would be followed by more lies. Before the nice house, cars and beautiful clothes, Trinity and Derek lived many places; but no matter where they lived hell always followed.

While Trinity was still living with her parents, she became pregnant with their first daughter, Talimah. Pregnant, sixteen years old and unmarried was not what her parents had hoped for, but her mother dared not to complain too much because she had teenage secrets of her own. Trinity's father was always a quiet, observant man who didn't like chaos. He never liked Derek because wherever Derek went, chaos followed.

Derek left for the Army before he and Trinity got married and one month before Talimah was born. That was a scary time for Trinity because Talimah was born prematurely and had to be put in ICU. However, Trinity was getting paid child support because Derek was in the Army. Since she was receiving back pay in child support, her mother wanted every dime of it. Trinity had already given her mother her first check for household bills, which was $3,000.00, but her mother wanted the last check too, which was about $1,750.00. *She is so damn greedy*, thought Trinity. Trinity decided she'd had enough and she was not giving it to her. She couldn't believe her mother was so money hungry.

"I'm not giving you another damn dime!" Trinity shouted at her mother.

"Oh you're going to give me that money or your ass is out of here," her mother replied. At that point, Trinity and her mother began to fight. They were actually throwing blows and Trinity's father just sat there and did nothing. After that, Trinity moved in with a friend who helped her with whatever she needed. It was better than living at home and having her family judge her with their comments and dissatisfied looks.

When Derek returned from the Army, he and Trinity went to get their marriage license, but they had to take Trinity's parents with them because she was only seventeen. Trinity, Derek and Trinity's mother, Delores went inside the courthouse while Trinity's dad waited in the

"WHY"

car. He hated Derek. When they got down to the clerk's office and filled out the application for the marriage license, the truth came out. Derek gave the clerk his I.D. but it was bleached out. The clerk looked puzzled because the birth year that Derek put down on his application was different than what was on his license.

"Sir, your license says 1966, not 1976," he said. But Derek denied it. So the clerk looked at Trinity and asked, "Ma'am, do you want to proceed?"

Delores looked at her daughter and asked the same thing. Trinity, being ever so trustful, said, "No, I saw his birth certificate and his immunization card. He's telling the truth."

When they got in the car and Trinity's father heard what happened, he was so pissed and drove off so fast, his glasses slid off of his face. Trinity wanted to laugh, but she knew now was not the time. Not long after that, she and Derek had their wedding at the church and the rest is history.

Not too long after Derek got out of the Army, he and Trinity began having problems. Trinity knew they couldn't stay at her parents' house, so the next best thing was to leave with Derek. Embarrassed, bruised, seventeen and now a mother herself, Trinity moved in with Derek at his mother's house on the South Side of Chicago. She had never felt so alone. Trinity went from living with her parents to living in a two-family flat, infested with rats and roaches. Trinity was a long way from home and not used to living like this. They lived with Derek's mother for about six months. Derek's mother was upstairs and Trinity and Derek lived downstairs. That was a trip in itself. Although Derek's mother tried to stop her son from beating Trinity, she couldn't protect her all the time. The abuse never stopped. It wasn't enough for Derek to physically abuse her, but he went as far as throwing one of their kid's shitty diapers in Trinity's face. It wasn't just physical abuse; it was mental abuse as well. Trinity remembers waking up to Derek standing over her one night, watching her as she slept.

"What are you doing Derek?" Trinity asked.

"I'm trying to figure out a way to kill yo ass and get away with it," he replied.

(Fairytale Husband)

"Shut up, demon," Trinity said as she rolled over and went back to sleep.

These were just a few of the many ways Derek tortured Trinity, and all she could do was ask God, "why?" During one of their heated arguments, Derek spit on Trinity, which wound up becoming a habit. It got so bad that Derek would spit on Trinity every time he left the house. "This is what I think of you, you no good bitch," Derek would say before proceeding to spit on her. Usually, after Derek would spit on Trinity, she would say, "Well they spit on Jesus." Then, she would pray, cry and ask God, "*Why? Why God are you allowing this to happen to me? I am your daughter. This is supposed to be your son. Why is he doing this to me?*" Trinity would always ask this as she cried herself to sleep.

But one night, Trinity was not having it. She had braced herself for the spit. In her mind, this was going to be the last time he would spit on her. She knew it was going to be a fight, but she didn't care — she was ready. As Derek spit on her tear-stained face, Trinity spit right back on him and yelled, "Come on, come on, do it again!" Surprisingly, Derek did nothing. He just stood there in shock, walked away and stayed gone for the entire evening. Trinity was so proud of herself. It would be years before she would leave Derek, but she realized that night that a person only does what you allow them to.

"Hey, Trinity, I need to use your car," said Derek. Trinity loved that car — it was her first one.

"The keys are on the kitchen table," Trinity replied. Hours went by and Trinity began to get worried. It wasn't like Derek to skip dinner, but on the other hand, things had not been that great between them lately. Day turned into night and still no Derek. Trinity didn't know whether to call the police or her family. She didn't want to tell her family because they already didn't like Derek; especially her father.

"Hey, baby, I'm home!" Derek shouted.

Trinity came running down the hall. She was terrified and relieved at the same time. "Where were you, why didn't you call me?" Trinity asked.

"Ah, baby, I would have but I had to burn your car. I got sleepy at the wheel and hit someone. I think it was a person or a deer, and I was scared so I had to burn it," said Derek.

"WHY"

"Wait, what? Burned up my car?" Trinity was shocked. She ran to the door to look and sure enough, her car wasn't in the driveway.

Trinity didn't know a lot about cars, and she didn't believe him because she knew Derek was jealous that she had a car. She was just glad that he was home and he was okay. All she could do was hug and kiss him.

"I'm just glad you're okay, baby. I was worried about you. You're more important to me than some old car," Trinity told Derek.

Derek couldn't believe Trinity believed him. He looked at her in amazement. For a quick second, he felt bad for lying to Trinity. He couldn't believe how much she trusted him. The next day, Trinity told her father what happened to the car.

"He told you what?!" Trinity's father yelled.

"He told me he had to burn up the car because it was running hot and smoking," said Trinity.

"That lying nigga could've gotten the radiator and the engine fixed, Trinity," her father said. "He just didn't want you to have that car. Wait until I see his lying ass! I'm going to burn his ass up; see if he likes that!" After Trinity sat and thought about it, she knew Derek was lying. *Why God? Why do I let him treat me this way?*

She was a prisoner in her own home. She couldn't go anywhere and she barely had any friends. One day, Trinity was just tired of it all and needed a break from everything and everyone.

"Yeah, girl, I'll come and get you. I'm on my way," her friend Connie said. Before Trinity and Connie could get their hang on, Trinity needed to drop the kids off with Derek. He was over the Pastor's house with the deacons from the church.

"Okay cool, I just have to drop the kids off with Derek," Trinity told Connie.

"Girl, don't you think that nigga gon' start tripping cause you dropping off them kids?" Connie asked.

"Girl I don't care, I'm dropping them off anyway. He'll just be pissed," Trinity said.

"What the hell you mean can I watch the kids while you out with your friends?" Derek said. "Hell naw, yo ass shouldn't even be out of the house."

(Fairytale Husband)

Derek was walking over to Trinity, so she picked up Tiffany thinking he wouldn't hit her with the baby in her arms, but she was wrong. Derek hauled off and socked Trinity so hard that he busted her lip wide open. Trinity ran in the house to get the pastor and the deacons thinking they would help, but they didn't do too much of anything. Derek told them that she fell and they just looked at her like they didn't know who to believe. Trinity left the kids and jumped in the car with Connie.

"I'm sick of this shit! I'm leaving his ass," said Trinity. Trinity was gone for three days. She did go to the hospital, but she lied and told the nurse that she fell. When were the lies going to stop? She was convinced that no one knew but people suspected. During those three days that Trinity was gone, Derek managed to threaten and piss off all of her friends, so she decided to go back.

"He's gonna wind up killing you one day," Connie told Trinity.

Trinity wondered what kind of life she was living. What was all of this for? The money, the house, the clothes — none of that mattered anymore. But she knew if she tried to leave, Derek would try to kill her. Little did Trinity know, it would be a long time before she could stop running.

How could a man of God do these things to me? Trinity thought. *He's supposed to love me.* Eventually, Trinity wound up leaving Derek again and she needed a place to stay. After talking to Deacon Roy, he told Trinity that she could stay at his house. Deacon Roy served in the church that Derek pastored. Trinity knew Derek would be angry with her for accepting help from the deacon, but Trinity was desperate.

The deacon stayed downstairs while Trinity and her children stayed upstairs. Deacon Roy had a round build, wore glasses and was bald. He was a nice man. Derek was the pastor of the church, which is why the deacon and the other board members tried to keep the abuse a secret from the church. They tried to talk with Derek and help him with his marriage, but there was a demon attached to Derek that just wouldn't let him go. And unfortunately for Deacon Roy, everything came to a head when the deacon tried to stop Derek from beating Trinity.

"WHY"

"Man, get out of here! This is none of your business," Derek screamed at Deacon Roy.

"I'm just trying to help you, son. You can't love a woman and beat her with your fists; she's your wife," said Deacon Roy.

"Man, if you don't get the hell outta here I'm going to beat your ass," Derek told the deacon. But the deacon just couldn't stand by and let Derek beat Trinity, so he stepped in again and that's when Derek punched Deacon Roy. All Trinity could do was yell for Derek to stop. She felt so bad for the deacon because all he had ever tried to do was help her and her children. Now he was lying on the ground with a bloody nose. Derek fled the house before the police came, but the damage was done. Trinity had to move again, and unfortunately, it was back with Derek.

Derek had the whole congregation fooled. They thought he was such a loving husband. What they didn't know was that Trinity had to wear certain clothes just to cover up her bruises.

Why is Derek taking so long to preach? Trinity wanted to get home. She was tired and the children were tired. As if preaching a whole hour past their usual time wasn't enough, now he was talking to the other ministry departments. *Oh God. Here comes Sister Isabel*, thought Trinity. *I wonder what she wants.*

"Lady Trinity, you are so lucky to have a husband like Pastor Derek," said Sister Isabel. "I wish I had a man like him."

All Trinity could say was thank you, but she was living a lie — and Sister Isabel didn't have a clue.

"Mom, can we go yet? The church is almost empty." Trinity's son Derek Jr. said.

"Let me go ask your dad," said Trinity. Trinity hated interrupting Derek.

She knew what the consequences might be, but she didn't care. She was tired and ready to go home.

"Excuse me," Trinity said to Derek. "I was wondering if you know how much longer you're going to be. The children are tired."

(Fairytale Husband)

Derek turned around and gave her a warning look. Thank God one of the deacons came out before Derek could say something because Trinity could tell he was getting ready to go off.

"Hey, Pastor, are you on your way out because I wanted to lock up," he said.

"Yeah, man, we were just on our way," said Derek.

Trinity was so relieved that the deacon came in but he could not save her for what was about to happen in the car.

"Bitch don't you ever ask me if I'm ready to leave! I'll leave when I'm good and damn ready. Where the hell you gotta go, huh?" As Derek hauled off and slapped Trinity, he said, "You ain't got nowhere to go. See, its hoes like you that make a nigga want to backslide and lose it."

Poor Trinity just sat there, tears rolling down her face as their children watched. She was so hurt and embarrassed. The children knew not to say anything; they were used to it. They loved their father, but they were sick of him beating their mom and they were tired of watching her take it. *Sister Isabel thought I was the lucky one. If she only knew the hell I was going through. I wouldn't wish this life on anybody*, thought Trinity. *She is the lucky one.*

***

"Derek, please don't eat the greens. Let's save them for when we get over to Mama's house," said Trinity. It was Thanksgiving and they were going over to Trinity's mother's house for the holiday.

"What did you say to me, bitch? Don't tell me what to do!" Derek yelled. The next thing Trinity felt was her head hit the hardwood floor, hard! So hard that she must've passed out because when she finally came to, Derek was holding Tiffany and standing over Trinity yelling.

"Wake yo ass up, you stupid bitch. Yo dumb ass better not die on me!" Trinity tried to get up, but she was too groggy because she felt her head hit the floor again. When she woke up the next time, Talimah and Derek Jr. we're standing over her screaming and crying while Derek was still holding Tiffany and pacing the floor yelling at Trinity to get up.

"WHY"

"I ought to kill you and if you pass out on me again. That's just what I'm going to do, with yo' simple ass!" Derek shouted. "I SAID GET UP!!!"

As Trinity scrambled to get up, her head throbbing, her children crying and Derek still threatening to kill her, she knew she better not say a word. She got up slowly, managed to get to the bathroom and get herself together. Trinity's poor babies — they were so small at the time.

"Hurry up and get yourself together so we can go," Derek said. "Don't have me waiting all day. No apology, nothing. All Trinity wanted to do was take some aspirin and go to bed. But that was not going to happen. One thing she learned was never to put Derek in a situation that could possibly make him look bad. So, off to Trinity's mother's house they went. Pretending they were a happy family. Trinity's whole life was nothing but a lie.

Because she was raised to stand by her husband, to Trinity that meant taking any abuse from her husband for the sake of their marriage. Her mother and father had been together through good and bad, and her granny had survived after she and Trinity's grandfather had separated. Trinity knew her grandfather used to beat her grandmother. She had heard the stories about how her grandfather threw a brick at her granny and bust her head wide open. Trinity's mother had to call the police to stop her grandfather from beating Trinity's granny to death.

Trinity's mother saw her own mother getting beat all of her life, just like Trinity's children saw her being abused. All Trinity knew how to do was survive, but she couldn't help but wonder when this vicious cycle would end. She wished she had the courage to ask her mother, but she knew her mother would never tell her anything that made her or their family look bad. She couldn't ask granny because her precious granny was gone. If she could just have the courage to talk to somebody then maybe she could get some help.

Trinity had taken so many beatings — beatings while pregnant and beatings when she wasn't pregnant. Trinity got beat so much that she had to think about which bruises came from where. A lot of the beatings seemed to come when she was pregnant with their third child,

(Fairytale Husband)

Tiffany. One day while pregnant with Tiffany, Trinity was sitting on the couch and Derek came up and started choking Trinity for no reason.

"Bitch, I hope I choke you so you'll hemorrhage to death and die," he told her.

One time, Trinity was sitting on the couch reading her Bible and Derek walked right up to her and slapped her. "Dumb bitch, I don't want to be married anymore," he said. As he began to light the fireplace, he started taking family pictures and their marriage license, and threw it into the fire. All Trinity could do was cry and wonder what she did to deserve this.

Another time, again while she was pregnant with Tiffany, they got into another argument. "Derek, stop, what are you doing?!" Trinity screamed. Put it down, put it down!" Derek had picked up the headboard to their bed and was getting ready to throw it at Trinity. Trinity started running down the stairs to try and get away but the headboard hit her leg. "Derek, stop, I didn't do anything. I didn't do anything," Trinity pleaded. It was late and the children were asleep, so the last thing Trinity wanted to do was wake them. They had experienced enough of their father beating their mother.

"Shut the hell up! I'll do what I wanna do, bitch!" Derek ran downstairs after Trinity and cornered her. "I should go ahead and kill yo' ass, you dumb, stupid bitch! I wish you would just die," said Derek.

In that instant, something came over Trinity and she calmly quoted the scripture, "To be absent from the body is to be present with the Lord."

"Go ahead and kill me, Derek, I don't care anymore," she said. "I'm tired of you always beating on me, so go ahead and kill me." Trinity was done; she couldn't fight anymore. She wanted to die. Derek looked at Trinity with rage in his eyes, but at that moment he could do nothing but walk out. He just left. Trinity slid to the floor and began sobbing. It seemed like she cried for hours. When she finally got up to go to bed, she saw her sweet baby Talimah praying. Praying for her?

No four year old should have to go through that. No child should get awakened to their father beating on their mother and threatening to kill her. Talimah probably heard everything, thought Trinity.

"WHY"

"Mommy, are you okay?" Talimah asked.

"I'm okay baby. Don't worry about me. Let's just get you back into bed," Trinity said. She sat there on Talimah's bed looking down at her, wondering what was going to happen. Parts of her wanted to die, and she felt guilty about that because of her children. But parts of her knew she had to fight to stay alive for her children. She couldn't leave them alone and she definitely couldn't leave them alone for Derek to raise. *Why do I have to keep fighting? Why can't I just live in peace and sleep peacefully?*

Trinity liked singing. She especially liked the song **"Lean on Me"** by Bill Withers. **"Sometimes in our lives, we all have pain, we all have sorrow. But if we are wise, we know that there's always tomorrow. Lean on me, when you're not strong and I'll be your friend. I'll help you carry on. For it won't be long 'til I'm gonna need somebody to lean on."** Singing that song made Trinity feel good because it gave her hope.

"What the hell you singing that song for?" Derek shouted. "Ain't nobody helping you and I'm the only person you got, so shut the hell up cause ain't nobody coming to help you!"

Not only had Derek beaten her through the years, but he took her joy. He took her music and her ability to feel that she deserved to be free.

"No one should be allowed to do that to a person, right? God, your word says that you died for us so that we could be set free. Well Lord, help me, please," cried Trinity. "Help set me free!"

CHAPTER 5

(My Sister's Keeper)

"HEY, TASHA!" TRINITY yelled, "Come and go outside with me to play jump rope."

Tasha loved hanging with her big sister; even though they were only ten months apart. Trinity was Tasha's hero. What Tasha didn't know was, Trinity didn't want to jump rope with her. She was just keeping an eye on Tasha so she wouldn't be harmed by her cousin. The night time was the worst.

"Put the pillow between your legs," Trinity told Tasha. "It'll make the pain go away." As much as she tried to, Trinity just couldn't save her baby sister. As Trinity lay in bed, she tried to remember when it all started. When did the pain, the secrets and the shame begin? She had so many memories of pain that it was hard for her to make sense of it all.

Trinity was good at protecting her sister. She loved her and would do anything for her. That's one of the things she prided herself on being good at. But as good as she was at protecting her sister, she wasn't good at protecting herself. *Who's going to protect me?* Trinity thought.

"Get away from me, you slut!" Trinity yelled at Tasha. Tasha looked at Trinity like she wanted to cry. It was hard to believe that Trinity always looked out for her when they were younger. Now it seemed like all she did was call Tasha out of her name.

"Stop calling me that," Tasha replied. Why are you so mean to me? I haven't done anything to you."

"Yes you did! You went and got pregnant, hoe! Trinity said. "You went out and spread your legs, now you're pregnant."

(My Sister's Keeper)

Trinity was angry at her sister for getting pregnant. She had protected her all of her life and now at fifteen, her little sister was pregnant. Even though Trinity was only sixteen, she felt like Tasha was her daughter because their mother was never around to protect them. Trinity and Tasha's father were furious, while all their mother could talk about was what people in the neighborhood and church would say. It was a mess and Trinity had no sympathy for Tasha. She hurt Tasha on purpose; the sister she fought for, protected and loved. When Tasha needed her most, Trinity turned her back on her.

"You act like I did this on purpose. I didn't mean to get pregnant. I just wish I could get rid of it," Tasha said. "Yeah, well, you can't so you're just going to have to deal with it," said Trinity. Trinity didn't want Tasha to go anywhere with her, she didn't want to be seen with her. *I looked after her time and time again, and she goes and does this to me*, thought Trinity. Trinity was hurt and just wanted so much more for her sister.

Although Trinity was only sixteen, she was wise beyond her years. She knew she was treating Tasha badly, but she was just so angry with her. Trinity didn't realize it then, but she would soon learn a powerful lesson about forgiveness and not judging others. Tasha was Trinity's best friend and Trinity would soon need Tasha more than she knew.

Where is that crying coming from? Tasha wondered as she rushed downstairs. She heard crying but she didn't know where or who it was coming from. She soon found out who the source was: Trinity.

"Trinity, why are you crying?" Trinity couldn't talk. She just looked up at Tasha. How could she tell Tasha what had happened? "Trinity, talk to me. Tell me what's wrong," pleaded Tasha.

After all the terrible names Trinity had called her, Tasha was still there for her; concerned about her. "Trinity, tell me what's wrong. Whatever it is we can get through it together," said Tasha. Sobbing, Trinity looked up at Tasha. She could barely speak. If only she hadn't said all of those things to Tasha; she didn't want to be called a hypocrite. This was the day Trinity learned never to judge anyone.

She put her head down in shame and whispered, "I'm pregnant too."

CHAPTER 6

(Trinity's Best Friend)

LIFE CAN BE unbearable sometimes, but it can also be made sweet by honest love and friendship. That's what David provided for Trinity. He was kind, not shallow. He fought for what and whom he believed in. He was a man's man. He wasn't a punk, and that turned Trinity on. She knew she had a good one this time. When he held her, she felt secure. She gave him anything he needed, and David gave just as well as he got. They had become fast friends and once again, Trinity tried to seek out a life of normalcy but that too would not last.

They didn't meet in a traditional sense. They met on the Internet, but that's not what they told everybody because they were embarrassed. Their first date was at a local jazz club. Neither one of them knew what to expect. He was looking for somebody he could play with and Trinity was looking for somebody to pay her bills. They were both hustlers who came with the intention of gaming one another.

"You're looking lovely tonight," said David.

"You're looking pretty fly yourself," Trinity replied.

David was a pretty boy with a fly suit, and the hat and shoes to match.

"So what does it take to make a beautiful woman like you happy?" David asked.

"Well, that depends. Tell me what you think will make me happy and I'll tell you if you're hot or cold," Trinity said, giggling.

She knew a player when she saw one because she was one. Never give them a straight answer, always keep them guessing and whatever you do, always stay in control. David was thinking the same thing. *This*

(Trinity's Best Friend)

chick is trying to play me, he thought. But he liked it. He liked a challenge and Trinity gave him one.

One date turned into two. Their second date was at the casino and Trinity noticed that David always wore suits, which Trinity knew was typical of a player, but she would soon be in for a surprise. She liked David and she knew he liked her. They eventually put their hustle mentalities aside and just concentrated on getting to know one another.

David and Trinity's third date was a night filled with drinks and love-making. Trinity couldn't find a babysitter that night, so David came over. Trinity was so excited that she answered the door in a sheer nightie with nothing wrapped around her but a sheet. She wanted David and she knew he wanted her to.

"Damn, yo ass is looking good," David said when Trinity opened the door.

After a several drinks, Trinity began to ask David questions. She felt something was up with him, more than he was letting on.

"Are you saved?" Trinity asked.

"Yeah, I'm saved," replied David. She wanted to know more.

"Do you believe in the laying on of hands, do you speak in tongues?"

David was getting aggravated by all the questions and answered Trinity with a quick "Yeah I do, now let's leave it alone." Trinity left it alone for now because she wanted to make love to David and she knew he wanted her too. Besides, all the wine they had been drinking made it very easy to seduce one another. Before she knew it, David's hands were all over her and she was all over David. They spent the next few hours making each other scream. Trinity had never felt this way about anybody before. She finally felt like she didn't have to pretend with him. She could be herself, she could be honest, she could be flawed and David would still want and love her. Why? Because in more ways than one, David and Trinity were alike — they both lived double lives that no one knew about.

The next time they were together Trinity just couldn't help that nagging feeling that David wasn't telling her everything, so she began asking more questions. She asked about his church and if he had a position in the church. To her surprise, David not only ministered, but

"WHY"

he was a pastor! Trinity was so shocked and excited because all of her life she knew she was supposed to do great things for the Lord and that her husband was supposed to be a man of God. This was it! God had finally blessed her with her happily ever after! But she was worried because she didn't feel like she was spiritually worthy of David. *God, I don't think I'm enough, I'm not worthy of this man,* Trinity would often say to herself. *And I am not right, right now.*

One night while they were making love David said, "I love you and I want you to be my wife."

"Oh, I love you too," said Trinity. This was Trinity's happily ever after, her dream come true. But, Trinity was scared to become a first lady with all the responsibilities it would bring. *Again, will I be good enough? Will I be pretty enough? Will I hear from God?* Trinity had so many questions, but she would soon find out that her life as a first lady would involve nothing the Bible ever spoke of.

"Hey, mom and dad, I'm engaged," Trinity told her parents. Trinity's parents had never even met David. Trinity also wasn't divorced from Derek yet — her and Derek's son "J" was only a year and half old at the time. But here she was, in love and ready to take the plunge again. They met a week after Valentine's Day, got engaged in October of the same year, and married in June of the following year.

They had a beautiful church wedding. David was a man of God that everyone loved. David was a worshipper who cradled God in his spirit, and Trinity was a prayer warrior. They made a perfect match, she thought. Her grandmother had taught her how to pray and worship early in life so she was confident in that, but holding the title of First Lady was different this time. Unlike Derek, David wanted Trinity involved in the church instead of just sitting on the pew looking cute. Trinity got ordained with David when she was twenty-eight. *He's perfect,* Trinity thought. *He's everything I've always wanted in a man.* David wasn't perfect — no one is — but for now, he was perfect for Trinity.

"Oh my God, David!" Trinity screamed. "Where did you get all of this money?!"

While they were dating, David always wined and dined Trinity and he spoiled Trinity's children. They went on trips and stayed at The Ritz-Carlton, among other fancy hotels. It was nothing for him to buy

(Trinity's Best Friend)

her Versace purses and Cartier necklaces and whatever else she or her children wanted. David was family-oriented and he loved Trinity and her children very much.

And then one day, he dropped $50,000 on the bed. Trinity had never seen that much money before. She never questioned David because she knew that he was a successful mortgage broker. As a matter of fact, he had several businesses, so this money had to be legit. Right? Trinity had been around her share of wealthy men and she knew David was a hustler. Hell, she was one to, but she had no idea just how much of a hustler David was.

"Don't worry about where I got this money, David replied. "It's ours and you don't have to dance anymore." David didn't like Trinity dancing so he shut all of that down. Trinity was now 25 and had been dancing for a year when they met. She even kept dancing after her son "J" was born. She was leading a double life because low-key, Trinity loved to dance. But anything that had to do with other men could be dangerous for Trinity. David was very jealous and he didn't like anybody talking to Trinity or even looking her way, especially when he got drunk. Trinity didn't know how jealous David was until one night when they were out at the club.

"Yo, who the hell you looking at nigga? That's my woman!" David shouted at some random dude.

He almost got into two fights that night because other guys were looking at Trinity, even though he knew she wasn't going home with any of them; he still couldn't handle it. When they got in the car to go home, Trinity noticed something was a little off with David.

"Babe, are you okay to drive?" Trinity asked. As usual, David thought he was okay to drive when he was drunk.

"Are you sure? Because I could drive home."

"I said I'm good." But he wasn't. David drove so fast that Trinity wasn't even drunk anymore. Her buzz was long gone and she was scared as hell!

"David, baby please slow down. You're scaring me," Trinity pleaded. "What about the kids if something happens to us?" Just let me out!"

David did just that; he let her out in an alley.

"Get out," yelled David. "Get the hell out of my car!"

"WHY"

Trinity got out, but she was so pissed and fed up with David. *We can't even go out without this nigga always going off*, she thought. Now she was all the way on the south side of town, in an alley, with no cell phone because it was still in the car. She just began to pray. All of a sudden, she saw this car speeding up to her, but it was coming in reverse. It was David. He had come back.

"Get in the car!" David yelled. "God yelled at me to come back and get you. This was the first time I heard God yell." David said that God told him, "What are you doing? Go back and get my daughter." Trinity didn't know what to think or feel. All she could say was thank you Jesus. Prayer works. David moved over and let Trinity drive. He had the nerve to sleep all the way home like nothing had even happened.

This may sound strange, but for the most part, they were a happy family. A family that was creating lots of memories. But something was missing. Even though David had a son from his previous relationship, he wanted to have a baby with Trinity. But for whatever reason, he didn't think he could have any more children. Trinity wanted a child with David too, so she began to pray. One thing Trinity had the utmost faith in was her ability to pray fervently. Her prayers didn't go unanswered. Within one month, she and David would be expecting their first child together. This would be number five for Trinity and she couldn't have been happier. But little did she know, there was a storm coming and its name was "David!"

"Please give me the knife, baby, please don't do it," David said.

"Fuck you, David! I'm sick of this shit and I'm sick of you! Trinity yelled.

Trinity ran into the kitchen to get a knife so she could stab herself. She didn't really want to hurt herself, but she was just so sick of David's shit. Earlier that day, Trinity got a phone call that set her off in the worst way and she just wanted to end it all.

"Yeah, I'm looking for Dee?" Dee was David's street name, but why was this woman calling David's phone?

"Who are you?" Trinity asked

"I'm Dee's girlfriend. Who are you?"

(Trinity's Best Friend)

"I am his wife," Trinity replied. "If you're his woman and y'all sleep together, what does his penis look like? *If this bitch answers this question correctly, I'm going upside David's head,* Trinity thought to herself.

Trinity marched into the bedroom yelling, "Get up! Get up David! Wake yo ass up!"

"What the hell is wrong with you, woman?!" David yelled back.

"I thought you told me that you were only selling dope out of that fat white bitch's house, so now I find out that you're sleeping with her too? What kind of shit is this?"

"I love you baby. I swear she doesn't mean anything to me. It's only head. I only let her give me head," David replied; as if that was okay.

"I thought you loved me! What about me, what about us?" Trinity cried. "All you do is lie. You're nothing but a liar! I hate you!"

Trinity then called David's mom, and while David's mom was hollering at her son on the phone, Trinity went into the kitchen and grabbed the knife and through the grace of God, David stopped her.

But David almost didn't get out of the bedroom to save Trinity. When he finally calmed Trinity down, he told her there was a pack of greyhound dogs that wouldn't let him leave the bedroom. Trinity knew he was talking about demons, David was spiritual like that. He had a gift and no amount of sin could take it away unless God took it away.

The next morning, while Trinity was in the shower, she looked down and saw chunks of blood everywhere. Trinity was having a miscarriage. Even though she was calm, Trinity's soul was in agony, so much so that she went into David's stash of pills and pulled out some OxyContin. Trinity wasn't planning on taking it but she did lick it a few times, enough to feel woozy and enough to get David hysterical again. Trinity just wanted him to see what his lifestyle was doing to her and their family, so going off and creating dramatic circumstances was her only weapon.

Here she was, pregnant with her fifth child, still in her twenties and in love with an absolute fool! They were only married for a year, but Trinity was a trooper. She believed in the sanctity of marriage and she knew in spite of all his flaws, David loved her. He was her best friend, right? Trinity believed she could love all of David's flaws away. *He'll love*

"WHY"

me and the kid's enough to change. Help him, Lord. Help my husband, Trinity would pray. But he didn't change — he got worse. Even though he was a Pastor, he had issues and hid them behind the pulpit.

When David's friend died, Trinity knew David was upset over his death, so she thought she would make a nice intimate evening for the two of them. She put on her lingerie, ran the Jacuzzi, made dinner and waited for her husband to come home from the funeral. David was gone all day. He called and said he was coming home, but he didn't. Instead, the next call Trinity got almost sent her over the edge.

"Hello, hello, David are you okay?" Trinity asked, but no one answered. It was obvious that David butt-dialed Trinity when she heard David's cousin, Marlow, in the background. Marlow was a minister at their church but what Trinity heard in the background was not sanctified at all.

"Yeah, Angela, get my cousin then get me. You know how I like it girl."

But that wasn't Marlow's voice, it was David's! They were with some hoe!!

> "Ooh shit, you give some good head girl. Damn, you gonna make me cum," said Marlow. "Hmmm, I'm ready for you, David. Are you ready for me?" Trinity heard the woman say. Then Trinity heard her husband making sounds that he should only be making with her.

Trinity cried so long and so hard that her feet began to hurt — pain, such unbearable pain. David had promised her that he would get his act together, but as usual, he lied. When Trinity saw David's cousin Marlow, she went off; especially since he was about to get married. Marlow begged Trinity not to tell his fiancé.

"I should tell her ass that you ain't shit," said Trinity. Meanwhile, David promised Trinity he would get clean. "Don't leave me, baby. I'll get clean, I promise. I love you. You will always be my wife," David told Trinity. That promise lasted six months.

Trinity called David's mother. She was the only person Trinity felt comfortable talking to about her and David's relationship.

(Trinity's Best Friend)

"I'm sorry honey, but that's what men do," was his mother's response. David's relationship with his mom got on Trinity's nerves. He always seemed to put his mother before Trinity and when Trinity would mention it to David, David would call Trinity controlling. She did, however, come over to the house the next day and cuss David out, but he denied all of it. Trinity didn't believe David's mom would do too much to get David to act like a husband; especially since he treated his mother more like his wife than Trinity. Once when David's mom was visiting, David started complaining about his back hurting and his mom got up and went into the kitchen to massage his back. Trinity told David that she was his wife and she should be massaging his back — not his mother.

"Woman, shut up with all that nagging. My mother can do what she wants," David replied.

It didn't make it any better that David's mother never corrected David. It was as if she wanted to be number one. David's sister Lois told Trinity that their mom always spoiled David. Lois hated that their mother favored David over her. When Lois was having problems with her husband, their mother barely lifted a finger to help.

"This is it! I can't it take anymore," Trinity told David. She was going to tell their pastor. David begged her not to go and asked the pastor to help save their marriage. He didn't want anybody to know how much of a creep he was. But it was too late. The church had already begun to suspect something — church folks are known to be in your business. Trinity always was taught to keep your dirty laundry inside the house and not outside so folks "could get a whiff." But this was something bigger than her keeping secrets. She had to tell her pastor because she had no one else to confide in. It was either tell someone or go crazy.

"I knew something was wrong with David, but I just couldn't put my finger on it. I knew he had been in trouble in the past, but I thought he was done with all that monkey business," said Pastor Jones to Trinity. "He's such a gifted and anointed man, I hate to see you both go through this, but as you know, until you both can be in a balanced state and right with God, I'm going to have to *sit you down*," he continued. "But I will talk with David if he'll listen, and I'm always here for you

"WHY"

both if you need me," said Pastor. "Sit you down" means you're relieved of all of your church duties. Trinity and David could no longer lead praise and worship, teach classes, or anything else.

So here was Trinity, exposed and feeling alone. David, who she thought was her fairytale husband, was an adulterer and also had a gambling addiction. Now she's in another broken marriage wondering which way to turn. David was still her hero. Trinity can remember once when she was going to her doctor's appointment to get her regular Pap smear, it came back abnormal. Trinity was so scared. All the indications showed it could be cancer, so the doctors did a biopsy to see exactly what was wrong. Trinity, who has always known the power of prayer, told David and he instantly began to pray. Trinity remembers that whatever it was she could feel it instantly leave, so when the doctors told her that all the tests were negative, she wasn't surprised. She knew how powerful prayer was and she knew how anointed her husband was. "So why God, why is this heartbreak happening to me again?" asked Trinity.

CHAPTER 7

(Red's Girl)

"I'M SICK OF living here! I just want to leave!" Tasha yelled. "I'm running away." "You're not going anywhere," her mother replied. "And if you do leave, don't come back."

Trinity and Tasha's mother Delores was very strict. She hardly ever let them do anything outside of going to church. The argument between Tasha and Delores was due to her mother's distrust of Tasha's male tutor. Tasha was a good girl, but her mother suspected otherwise. Even though Tasha was doing nothing wrong, her mother just didn't believe her. Delores was only trying to protect them. Later as grown women, Tasha and Trinity would realize that their mother was just trying to protect them from the hell they both went through as a child.

What is all the yelling about? Trinity wondered. She was watching television when she heard all of the yelling and ran to the front of the house to see what was going on. By the time she made it, all she saw was Tasha heading out of the door. Trinity tried to stop her, but Tasha had made up her mind that she was running away and there was nothing anyone could do about it.

"Y'all can go over to my cousin's house," said Betty, "I'll call y'all a cab." It was late in the evening and Trinity, fifteen, and Tasha, fourteen, had never been out walking in the neighborhood this time of night. Trinity tried everything to get her sister to go back home, but Tasha was determined to run away. They eventually found themselves at Betty's house. She was referred to as a "street girl" by Trinity. Even though Betty was just sixteen, Trinity never trusted her, but she knew Betty would probably be able to help them. That night, the cab took them to

(Red's Girl)

a house with a lot of men. No one there was under twenty-one. When the girls got in the house, one of the guys told them to go to the back room. The girls were nervous, but there was no turning back now.

As Trinity and Tasha made their way to the back room, Trinity couldn't help but think, *how in the hell did I get here?* Trinity knew how to survive at home, but this was unfamiliar territory. She didn't know anyone and she was slowly becoming convinced that Betty had set her and her sister up. She knew Betty couldn't be trusted, but they were here now, so she and Tasha had to protect one another.

"Take that nigga outside," a man named Mark yelled. He and his brother Coldwater were dwarfs and apparently they were in charge. "Bust a cap in that nigga," said another guy named Red. Red was the brothers' cousin, and he had his eye on Trinity as soon as she came into the room.

"Please don't shoot me, man," the guy pleaded. So instead, they stabbed him in the leg right in front of Trinity and Tasha. Trinity did not want to be a witness to anybody being hurt or possibly murdered, but she also knew she had to play it cool.

"Take his ass outside in the backyard," one of the brothers said.

"Trinity, I'm scared," Tasha whispered.

"Don't be scared, we'll be alright," Trinity assured Tasha — but she was scared herself.

"Here, put these on," said Red.

Later that night, he gave Trinity and Tasha long t-shirts to sleep in. Trinity liked Red and Red liked Trinity. They laid in the same bed and talked all night.

"Shit, I just wanna spend all my money on you girl," said Red. They talked about all kinds of stuff; she even told Red that she was still a virgin. While they were in the bedroom talking, one of the brothers was outside upset because he liked Trinity too.

"Mark told me the light-skinned sister was his, but shit I don't know. Both of y'all light-skinned to me," Red said while he and Trinity lay in bed.

Trinity thought her sister, Tasha was light-skinned, but not her. But none of that mattered because Red was fine. He was about six feet tall

"WHY"

with caramel skin, hazel eyes and pretty white teeth. She didn't mind lying next to him at all. The next day would prove to be a real challenge for Trinity and Tasha because the brothers had plans for the sisters — plans that would test both of the sisters' resolve. They didn't know it then, but the brothers and their mother were to be feared. Trinity lay in bed thinking, *God, why are we here? I'm only fifteen years old, what did I do to deserve this?*

She thought about all the times she wanted to get out of her mother's house, but she never thought she would be in a situation where she wished she were back at home. As Trinity was drifting off to sleep, she wished she could go back home and Red could come with her. He was the only man besides her dad and brother who was nice to her. Red made her feel protected — something she never felt before. Plus he was fine and she liked the way he touched her; it was different. He touched her like he cared about her instead of all the other times she had been touched.

Trinity knew they were going home — she could feel it — she just didn't know how. Would she or her sister get beaten up or raped? Would her face get messed up? Would her mother even want them back? What would her neighbors think? Would anybody else in the neighborhood know? She began thinking all these thoughts and she just wished this nightmare would soon be over. But she knew if she was going to get out of this, she would have to pray. Trinity knew when all else failed, she could pray. "Prayer fixes everything," her grandmother would always say. *Well Jesus, I need you to fix this and hurry up please!*

CHAPTER 8

(Granny)

TRINITY DIDN'T WANT to go shopping with her mother, but she knew if she went with her she would buy her stuff, so she tagged along. Her sisters were back at the house with her granny; she hadn't been feeling too well lately. Trinity liked having her granny around. She always spoke her mind and she didn't hold anything back. *She's a feisty old lady*, thought Trinity. She began thinking about how her granny first showed her how to worship.

"Trinity, come here. I want to teach you how to worship," Granny said. Trinity's grandmother, Grace, was the epitome of love in Trinity's life. Trinity was eleven or twelve when her grandmother taught her how to worship. At a young age, Trinity would cry and worship unto God, and her Granny would also wrap her in prayer clothes. Trinity was a prayer warrior at an early age, which is why she just couldn't understand why God would allow these terrible things to happen to her.

"Do you know how special you are?" Granny would say to Trinity. "God is going to use you mightily and you will have favor in His sight."

Even though Trinity usually believed whatever her grandmother told her, she didn't feel special — she felt dirty and ashamed. If her grandmother knew the things she had been doing to her brother's friends, she would be so disappointed in her. Trinity wanted to change and be different, but she didn't know how.

As long as Trinity could remember, Granny was always telling her how to do something or giving her pearls of wisdom.

"Never trust a man. Be independent," her grandmother would say. "Get a good education, so you can make good money." Trinity

(Granny)

admired her grandmother because she didn't take anything from anybody. Trinity's father even nicknamed her Joe Louis!

Trinity's grandmother was no saint back in the day. She had been raised on a plantation in Tennessee where she picked cotton. Grace and Trinity's grandfather, Aster, had been sweet on each other for a long time. Grace always talked about leaving Tennessee and doing something different.

"Aster, promise me that you'll take me away from all of this," Grace would say to him. "I want us to have our own business and a bunch of children."

Trinity's grandfather made good on his promises and he moved Grace and himself north to Chicago where they eventually started their own business and had nine children.

Trinity's grandfather was a handsome, dark-chocolate, muscular man who unfortunately used his strength to beat on Trinity's grandmother. Aster had served in WWII and suffered from mental and emotional trauma as a result of killing a lot of people during the war. He survived the war, but got injured badly. He would spend the rest of his life with a metal plate in his head.

"Hit me again and I'm gonna wear yo ass out!" Grace yelled."

"I'd like to see you try!" Aster yelled back."

When Grace's grandparents moved from Tennessee to the south side of Chicago in their twenties, they didn't use to fight. They loved each other deeply, but the war and the metal plate combined with Aster's drinking and drug abuse made for a volatile marriage. It also didn't help that Grace was no punk, and she challenged Aster and did what she wanted to do.

Trinity's grandmother was short, but she could pack a punch. Trinity came from a family of fighters and hustlers. Trinity grew up hearing stories of how her grandfather and her grandmother used to fight. Trinity remembered hearing stories about how her mother and her mother's brother, Uncle Mac, would beat up on their father because he would jump on their mother. Trinity loved her Uncle Mac. He was her favorite uncle because he always had something funny to say. He was charming, full of jokes and always stayed sharp. Uncle Mac was clean from head to toe. He always had his hair slicked back and he always

"WHY"

wore a sharp pair of shoes. But for most of Trinity's adult life, Uncle Mac had been in prison.

Even though Trinity came from a dysfunctional family, deep down they loved one another and had each other's back. There were times when Aster was a cold-hearted bastard to Trinity's grandmother and there were times when he was a hero. Trinity remembered her mother telling her a story about how her girlfriend was constantly being raped by her own father. She said she told Trinity's grandfather and he went over there and, let's just say her girlfriend's father got handled in a manner that he would never see daylight again. Through the years, her grandparents fought and made up numerous times until Grace couldn't take it anymore. They eventually split, but Trinity's grandmother would live to see her ex-husband quit drinking, doing drugs and even receive Christ in his life as his personal savior. Trinity's grandfather Aster died from a stab wound to the neck. At the time, Trinity's mother said she had a vision of her father holding the side of his neck bleeding. Trinity was about ten or eleven years old when it happened.

Trinity's grandmother got her life together, accepted Christ as her Lord and Savior, and raised her children the best she could. Out of Grace and Aster's nine children, only two of Trinity's aunts and uncles remain alive today. Trinity's mother, Delores, and her brother, Uncle Mac, who remains in prison to this day. As years would pass, Trinity would come to understand why her mother was so hard on her and her sisters. Delores could only give of the little good that she got during her childhood, and she could only teach as her mother and father had taught her. In later years, Trinity would realize that her grandmother and her mother were taught to survive. They were taught how to fight and how to stay alive. It would be up to Trinity to change this vicious cycle of secrets and abuse.

"Hurry up and come home! Something is wrong with Granny!"

That was the call that Trinity and her mother got while they were out shopping. What could be so wrong with granny to make her sister call like this? Trinity's mother Delores was scared. She had this look on her face as if she knew something bad happened, but Trinity could tell that her mother was trying to be calm. At the time, Trinity didn't know it, but she wouldn't see her grandmother alive again.

(Granny)

"Nooooo" Trinity yelled as she entered the house, "What happened?!"

Granny was laying on the bedroom floor with a sheet over her.

"Noooo, she's not dead. I see the sheet moving," cried Trinity. Trinity's father wrestled with Trinity until she calmed down. She just couldn't believe her Granny was gone. Before she and her mother arrived, Granny had died in Tasha's arms.

Tasha told Trinity that Granny was sick and she kept going to the bathroom on herself. "Every time I cleaned her up, she would poop again, so I went and got Dad and he called the ambulance."

Tasha told Trinity that granny kept talking to God and asking for His forgiveness.

I was too late. I could've saved her, thought Trinity. Granny had suffered from a previous fall and had developed a blood clot in her knee that moved to her heart, causing her death. Trinity's mother said, "God knew if Trinity and I were here we could've brought her back to life."

Strong faith was a staple in Trinity's household, and soon after Granny's death, Trinity became distant from God. She had lost hope. If only Trinity knew what all awaited her, she would've clung to her faith; but her pain was too unbearable. Who would tell her how special she was? Who would give her hope in God? Who would protect her from her mom? Granny had always been a buffer between Trinity and her mom, but now Trinity truly felt alone. Trinity had never experienced heartache like this before. She may have felt loss before, but this loss was pure. It came with a love that was not harmful, not judgmental and totally giving. She vowed that she would make her grandmother proud by getting a good education, continue reading her bible, and always pray and worship.

Granny had survived picking cotton, losing a business, enduring physical and verbal abuse by a man who said he loved her, being a single parent with nine children and being a black woman in America. *If Granny could survive all of that, surely I can survive the hell I'm going through,* thought Trinity. R.I.P Granny, I'll always love you.

CHAPTER 9

(First Lady by Day, Prostitute by Night)

AFTER TRINITY MOVED out of Deacon Roy's house, she and Derek moved into one of her aunt's properties. Trinity still hadn't found the courage to leave Derek for good. She loved him and she always wanted to believe he loved her and was a good person — even though she knew a person doesn't love you with their fists. About seven years had passed, Trinity was now twenty-three and she and Derek had three children together: two beautiful daughters and one son. Trinity was especially protective of her daughters; she dared not have them go through what she went through. Her hell was hers and hers alone, and no one would ever know or understand what she went through. On the outside, everything seemed to be perfect. Who would think the Pastor of the church would be her abuser and her "at-home pimp"? Trinity learned to survive the abuse by prostituting herself with her husband — First Lady in the day and at-home prostitute at night.

Trinity was starting to realize that for all the love and attention she gave Derek, she was still getting the short end of the stick. He was running around beating people up, beating her up and sacrificing their kids, for what? What was it all for and why was she still in love with him? Whenever she tried to love him and do nice things for him, he would agitate her and beat her down with his words. One time Trinity bought Derek a beautiful coat, not just because she loved him but also because she was tired of him wearing the same coat over and over again.

"Baby, look what I got for you", Trinity said to Derek excitedly. She couldn't wait to show him his new coat. She just knew he would like it.

(First Lady by Day, Prostitute by Night)

"What the hell is that?" Derek said. "I didn't ask you to buy me a new coat. The coat I have is good enough."

"I know honey, but I just thought you may like a new coat, that's all." What Trinity really wanted to say was "your old coat is torn, funky and everybody down at the church is talking about you," but instead her nice gesture turned into a screaming match. You would've thought Trinity cheated on Derek the way he was yelling at her.

As Trinity waited on tonight's bible study to be over, she found herself wandering in thought. She often thought of what it would be like to have a life of no pain caused by the people whom she trusted. This particular night, Trinity was eager to leave church because she was sore from the bruises her husband left on her back the night before when he forced her to have sex with him. He didn't hit her in the face because that would be too obvious. Derek didn't want his congregation to become suspicious. But there was no limit to what he would do to the rest of her body. Derek loved pastoring the church because he loved the attention. He beat Trinity because beating her kept her under control and Derek liked being in control. Trinity wondered what would happen when they got home from bible study. She just wanted to go home, put the kids to bed and go to sleep, but it was never up to her — it was always up to him. Would tonight be a night filled with much-needed rest or would he make her have sex with him? When they got home, Trinity put the kids to bed and tried to lie down, but Derek had different plans.

"Come over here and give me some head," Derek told Trinity.

"You got some money?"

Having sex with her husband was the only way Trinity could get money from Derek. When Derek could not pay, he took it. "Your body belongs to me and I can do whatever I want to it," he would say.

Trinity hated having sex with Derek. It reminded her of the movie "The Color Purple," where Miss Celie described her husband Mr. of "doing his business" on her; and it felt just like that. It didn't feel good at all. Ten minutes felt like ten hours.

"Lay yo ass still and don't move. If you know what's good for you, you won't move until I cum," Derek told Trinity.

"WHY"

She felt dirty, but she needed to survive another night without getting hit so she lay there until Derek was finished. As she turned over to get up to go in the bathroom to wash his smell off of her, she thought to herself, *I made it without getting hit tonight.*

During those years, Trinity's best friend Connie knew Trinity needed money and she knew Derek wasn't giving her any, so she turned Trinity on to dancing professionally.

"Girl, you better come on and get this money. All that ass you got, you could get paid," Connie said.

"I don't know girl. What if somebody at the church finds out? Better yet, what if Derek finds out? He's going to kill me," said Trinity.

"Girl, screw Derek! You already tricking for him anyway. You better get this money," said Connie. Besides, you ain't gon' be in a club. You'll be doing private parties."

"Alright, I'll think about it and let you know," Trinity replied. Trinity thought about it, but it didn't take long for her to make a decision. She had become used to life as a Pastor's wife and all the perks that came along with it. Even though she was in her aunt's house, it was a 3,000-square-foot home. She had the clothes, the cars and now she was about to make this money. *Why not?* Trinity thought. She had to get paid somehow. She figured she had been a good girl all of her life, and where did that get her?

CHAPTER 10

(Dope House Dancer)

THE NEXT DAY while her sister Tasha was back at the dope house, Trinity was taken to another one of the dwarfs' houses down the street. She wondered what was going on, but was too scared to ask any questions. When she got there she saw drug dealers, and the brothers' mother, who was also a drug dealer and a dwarf-like her sons. Her name was Rose, and she kept looking Trinity up and down like she was a piece of meat. She told her son Mark that she thought Trinity would do just fine. *Fine at what?* Trinity wondered.

Mark was one of the brothers that liked Trinity, and he was jealous and pissed that his cousin Red spent the night with her. Mark had suspected that Red had bust that cherry, and now Mark wanted Trinity even more. But first he would teach Trinity how to cut, cook, bag and sell his drugs. Just 24 hours ago, Trinity was at home with her family and now she was in a strange house dealing drugs. *Who's going to believe me when I get home?* Trinity wondered. In spite of everything Trinity still believed that she and her sister would be free to go back home.

Trinity didn't know that back at the other house Tasha was dealing with her own struggles. When Trinity got back to the other house, she heard some guy screaming, "I'm going to kill that bitch! She cut me, man!" Trinity noticed Tasha's clothes were torn and Tasha was crying. Trinity ran over to Tasha and asked, "What happened?" Tasha told Trinity that the guy tried to rape her three times and she stabbed him with some scissors in his leg.

"Trinity, I want to go home," Tasha whispered, "Please get us out of here."

(Dope House Dancer)

"Oh God, please help us," Trinity prayed. "Please get us out of here." God would get them out of there, but not yet. Trinity didn't know it but she soon would be the main attraction.

"Shake that ass, baby," yelled one of the men. Trinity was so nervous. She had never danced in front of men before and she couldn't believe that one of the men was a Deacon. He was the loudest one. *So much for being a man of God*, Trinity thought. *He's just like all these other guys.*

Rose had sized up Trinity earlier at the house because she knew she would be dancing that night. If Rose had it her way, Trinity and Tasha would be dancing for them every other night. Rose pimped out young girls, which is why Betty sent them over there. Trinity knew she shouldn't have trusted Betty. *Oh well*, she thought. She figured she had better dance because she was too afraid of what would happen if she didn't.

Trinity began drinking to take the edge off. She wondered if any other fifteen-year-olds were in a dope house dancing. Trinity soon began to get into it and even though she only had on her white t-shirt, bra and socks from last night, she danced like she had on a dancers outfit designed for her body. She was slanging that ass and dropping it to the floor. She let loose like something had been holding her back. Trinity may have only been fifteen, but she danced like a grown woman. Trinity always loved dancing and she knew how to entice men with her body. She knew what men liked because she had been taught what men liked at an early age. She knew if she was going to get out of this situation, she'd better dance like her life depended on it.

"Hey, little girl, come here," said one of the guys watching her dance. "You wanna make some more money?"

Trinity said yeah and the guy took Trinity into the basement. He told Trinity he would give her five hundred dollars if she let him have sex with her. Trinity low-key enjoyed the foreplay of it. *What's the big deal*, she thought. Plus she would be getting paid for it. Alcohol and Trinity's own sexual urges made her judgment not well thought out.

Trinity didn't know her sister Tasha was keeping watch over her. Tasha knew Trinity was drunk.

"Turn around so I can put it in," said the guy. Trinity turned around and pulled her panties down so he could put his dick in her but

"WHY"

it wouldn't fit. "Damn, you tight, girl," he said. This made him want Trinity even more.

"You must be a virgin," he said.

"Yeah, I am," answered Trinity. But for five hundred dollars, Trinity was willing to lose it to someone she didn't even know. He tried again, but his dick was just too big. So he told her, "Look, I'll just give you $200.00 for trying to let me hit it." Just as Trinity was pulling up her panties and putting her money in her sock, her sister Tasha and Red bust into the room.

"Get your hands off of her, man," Red said. "Trinity, what are you doing? Come on, let's go!"

Red snatched up Trinity and took her into the bathroom and said, "Isn't this enough for you? Why won't you let me hit it when I'm the one who cares for you?"

He then proceeded to pull his penis out of his pants so he could show it to Trinity. Tasha was more scared than anything. Trinity had always been her safety net. She wouldn't know what to do if something were to happen to her sister.

"C'mon, let's get back down the street," said Red. "You need to lay down."

Red had taken Trinity away from the party house because he knew what his cousins Mark and Coldwater were up to. Red knew as young and pretty as Trinity was, it would only be a matter of time before those dudes at the party would run a train on her. He knew that his cousin Mark was so pissed at him, he would let it happen. Mark wanted Trinity, but since his cousin Red had already made a play for Trinity, he backed off out of respect.

As Trinity, Tasha and Red made their way through a room full of strippers, Trinity slowed down to watch them dance. They seemed to be so free and sexual; all the things that Trinity wished she could be and have with someone who loved and not used her. When Trinity got back to the house, one of the twins took some of the money she made. She didn't care. She just wanted all of this to be over with so she could go back home.

I can't go through another night of this, Trinity thought. The next day, Trinity's prayers were answered. Red let Tasha use the phone to call

(Dope House Dancer)

their cousin and stood by her to protect her while she was using the phone. Tasha was so nervous. She didn't even remember her cousin Nikki's number, but God brought it back to her remembrance.

"Look man, if you ain't hitting that then she gotta leave. She gotta get the hell out of here," Mark yelled at Red. The brothers were pissed because they figured the police was going to come and arrest them, and Mark was even more pissed because not only did Red not get any pussy, but he didn't get any pussy either. The twins and their mother figured it was best to cut their losses and let them go.

"Get the hell outta here, and if either one of y'all says anything to anybody, I'm killing you and your whole family," said Mark.

At first the twins didn't want to let them out of the house, but Trinity and Tasha noticed their cousin Nikki's Durango going up and down the street, so they bolted out of the door. Nikki had her boyfriend with her, and he was a big buff dude. When the twins saw him get out of the truck, they didn't do anything. They didn't want any more trouble. Trinity and Tasha took off running down the street. They were never so happy to see anyone in their lives. When they got back to their cousin Nikki's house, Trinity's mother called. She told them that she was going to go to the news station but God put her cousin Nikki in her spirit, so that's why she called.

"Do we have to go back?" Tasha asked. "I don't want to get in trouble."

"Yes, we have to go back," Trinity replied. "We've been gone for five days." When they got back home, they just knew they would be in big trouble. They figured they would get whippings and be on all kinds of punishments.

"Where is all of our stuff?" Tasha asked Trinity.

"How am I supposed to know? I was with you, remember?" Trinity said sarcastically. Trinity was pissed. Someone had taken down all of their posters and everything else they had hanging on their walls. *Why, why would they do this*, thought Trinity? The girls not only didn't get a whipping but they were not put on any punishments. Nothing was ever said. It's as if it never happened. She couldn't understand why.

CHAPTER 11

(Trinity Meets the Husband She Prayed For)

WHO SAYS GOD doesn't answer prayers and dreams don't come true? What gives us the right to give up on ourselves? What gives us the right to not dream or not believe in a fairytale? So what if you've been hurt, so what if you've been married several times, what gives you the right to give up? Sometimes dreams do come true and prayer works!

His name was Chris and he was Trinity's covering, chosen by God. When God revealed to Trinity who she was, how worthy she was, she wasn't focusing on men or a fairytale husband; she was focusing on God. This time Trinity was concentrating on herself, but most importantly, she was focused on her children. As she began to appreciate her value as an individual and as a mother, she realized just how much her children needed her and how she had neglected them. She didn't mean to, it was just her life's journey at the time. Her children had all the material stuff but they hadn't had her presence. She was always in and out, working, in school, just trying to make a living.

Through the years, Trinity had amassed many degrees in spite of her life being in turmoil. While Trinity was with Derek, she graduated high school at seventeen earned her Associate's Degree in Liberal Arts and started college at nineteen, all while getting beat, getting pregnant and bearing four children.

When she was with David, she began working towards her Bachelor's degree in Business Administration with a minor in Computer Information Systems. She did this while dealing with a drug-addicted husband and getting pregnant three more times. All of this happened

(Trinity Meets the Husband She Prayed For)

over the span of five and a half years. But Trinity didn't stop there. She pursued her Master's Degree at twenty-seven while still with David.

Now that there was no more Derek and no more David, Trinity concentrated on getting healed from her abuses of the past. The last thing Trinity was looking for or wanted was another husband. She also wanted to make sure that she didn't get pregnant again, so after she left David, she got her tubes tied, cut and burned. *It'll be a cold day in hell before I get pregnant again*, thought Trinity.

Trinity may not have wanted any more children, but she still wanted her happily ever after with a husband. Even though she had been hurt, she still believed the Lord would send her husband. Before Trinity met Deacon Chris, she had spent time being alone, doing a lot of soul-searching and a great amount of healing. Not only was Trinity firmly planted in the church, but she was confident in herself. In the beginning of her journey to self-discovery, she didn't want another man. She just wanted more alone time with God. Trinity was so consumed with her children, her work and her duties in the church that it would have to be God himself to tell her that she would marry again. But Trinity was hopeful, which is why she still prayed.

Trinity knew the power of God's word and she knew she had to be specific in her prayers. The bible said God spoke the word and the world was formed. ***(Genesis 1:1-28), (Psalms 33:6)*** There were many scriptures referencing to the power of the tongue, but with that declaration of your mouth, you must have faith for your words to come to pass. ***(Hebrews 11:3), (Romans 10:17)*** Trinity knew all too well what it was like to have faith. Faith kept her sane and faith kept her productive through all the years of abuse. But mostly, faith kept her alive because she believed God had something better for her life.

"Lord, I know there is power in the tongue if I believe. Well God, I believe, so I'm putting my request in for a husband not only equipped by you but I'm asking for specific things as well." Trinity began to pray for a specific man because the word of God says to be specific in our prayers. **"Lord God I come to you in faith, that you would send me a**

"WHY"

man, a godly man that not only comes to church but has a relationship with you. Lord, I want him to be tall, older and brown-skinned. I want him to exercise and take care of his body. I want him to be a family man who loves children and Lord, if he has children, I would like them to be older if not adults. Lord, I pray that he is handy around the house and is capable of fixing things. I pray that he has his own business and is into landscaping because I love a beautiful yard. And lastly, Father, I pray he is a man who is content with being at home with his family, especially at night. Lord God, I pray all these things in Jesus' name, Amen."

Trinity had been praying that prayer for years since her divorce from David. She met other men, but she knew they were not her husband. She never gave up her faith. She continued to believe in the power of the tongue. It would be years later, but Trinity would preach on that very subject. Now all she had to do was wait and have the patience for God to do his great work.

It was at bible study when she first saw him. His name was Chris. Trinity didn't know it, but Chris was a well-respected deacon in the church. She couldn't help but notice how handsome he was, and he was also a little older. But she didn't pay him too much attention because she wasn't looking to date anyone. However, this was different. As much as Trinity tried to fight it, there was an attraction to this man. She couldn't put her finger on it, but it was as if it were meant to be.

Chris had joined the church three years before Trinity started going, and it was a whole year before Trinity actually met Chris. Trinity and Chris began their journey together before having ever met. Chris was invited to the church by family members, and Trinity was invited to the church by her girlfriend, who was the apostle's daughter. When Chris joined the church, the teaching was what he had been accustomed to. He needed to be taught and led by the Holy Spirit, not man's ego, and he found it at this church. Trinity got to the church by way of her ex-husband acting like a fool in the pulpit. She often asked herself why she was still going to this church anyway. They weren't together

(Trinity Meets the Husband She Prayed For)

anymore and it was all the way in Arlington Heights; thirty minutes from Chicago. She could have easily joined the church in the city. Trinity had been going back and forth from the church in Arlington where she was ordained as a minister, to her girlfriend's church in the city; she had been doing this for about two to three months. Trinity realized that no amount of saving face to her church family was worth being talked about, ordained minister or not. That wasn't God!

Trinity was in church with her children when David began to mention her and the children in a sermon and it was nothing nice. He had the nerve to say their children had demonic spirits in them just because they wouldn't sit still and look at him, and then he called her a Jezebel!

How in the hell are you going to be bashing me and my kids from the pulpit? Trinity thought. *Yo fake ass is still going to the strip clubs at night!* Trinity got her children and stormed out right in the middle of the sermon, and that was the last time she stepped foot in that church. She'd had enough! She had to learn to not care so much about what people thought about her and live her life according to God's instruction. Her entire life, Trinity had been raised to consider what other people thought. Her mother had drilled in her and her siblings' heads that they had to be or act better than other people. Failing or making mistakes wasn't an option in her household. Sadly, life isn't like that. It puts pressure on the children and sometimes can make them look down on others without dealing with their own flaws. This was a big step for Trinity, and she was proud of herself for walking out.

"Mama, where are we going?" DJ, her son asked.

"We're going to Pastor Kathy's church," Trinity replied. Trinity was tired of the back and forth anyway. It was time to sit down at somebody's church and get fed the true Word of God. Trinity's friend Kathy was the co-pastor whose mother, Apostle Love, was the head of the church. Trinity embraced the direction of the apostle, and she would always call Trinity to the altar to get delivered from something. Trinity didn't think she had so many unclean spirits on her, but Apostle knew. The years of abuse Trinity endured, manifested into witchcraft. Generational curses were being broken off of not only Trinity but her children as well. Apostle began to instill in Trinity that she was worth more than allowing herself to be abused by someone who cheated on

"WHY"

her and used drugs. Her life was more than that. Trinity needed to hear that. Even though she already knew it, she needed to feel that she was worthy.

Trinity and her children continued to go to Pastor Kathy's church faithfully, and it would be six months before Trinity and her children would join the church. She wasn't thinking about joining that day, but she felt the Lord urging her to go up during altar call, so Trinity and her son D.J went up to Apostle Love and joined. It was one of the happiest days in Trinity's life. She couldn't explain it, but she had a sense of peace.

"I want to join the praise team," said Trinity to Deacon Chris. Trinity immediately wondered why she told him that. Trinity had sung before and she knew she had a beautiful voice, but she was not trying to be on the praise team. It was as if the Lord pushed her to say that to Deacon Chris. That was the first time they spoke. Trinity knew she was under the authority of the Lord; He pushed her to say that. So now what?

"Mama, are you nervous? Trinity's daughter Tiffany asked. She was always watching her mom. She had a sweet spirit, she was passionate and creative.

"No, not really," Trinity replied. But she was nervous. The people at Trinity's new church had become her church family. They embraced her and her children, and Apostle Love even let Trinity keep her title of "Elder" when she joined the church. So why was Trinity so nervous?

"Alright, praise team, let's get ready to glorify the Lord. Let's sing praises unto His name," said the choir director. "We're gonna sing the roof off of this building today! We're gonna let the devil know that the Lord is mighty and victorious!"

This made Trinity even more nervous, but she couldn't turn back now. "Oh Lord, please cover my voice and help me remember all of the words," prayed Trinity.

When the praise team walked out and up to their mics, Trinity backed away from the mic because she was too nervous. She sang, but you could barely hear her.

Trinity felt so embarrassed, but Deacon Chris put her at ease.

(Trinity Meets the Husband She Prayed For)

"Look, don't beat yourself up. You did well and no one noticed because there were three other people on the mic with you. It's okay,' he said. "You being nervous is just a sign that you care and want to do well. I'd rather somebody like you sing for the Lord than someone who is arrogant and just wants to be seen."

Trinity thanked him and was getting ready to leave when Deacon Chris did something unexpected.

"Hey, Trinity, before you go, I was wondering if I could get your number? We can talk about it further and I can give you some tips to make you feel more comfortable on the mic," said Deacon Chris. But Deacon Chris had other things on his mind. Later that night, he sent Trinity a text asking her out, and she was shocked and speechless. She called Pastor Kathy, who always told her that God had a man "fashioned" just for her. Trinity asked Kathy what she should do.

"Kathy, you know I'm not trying to date anyone at the moment. Do you think I should go out with Deacon Chris?" Trinity asked.

"Girl, it's not like y'all getting married tomorrow," Pastor Kathy replied. "But if God chose this man to be your husband, then you do need to get to know him."

Trinity and Deacon Chris began talking on the phone and minutes turned into hours. They talked about everything. Their friendship was growing and Trinity was beginning to feel overwhelmed with emotional closeness to Deacon Chris.

Why am I feeling like this? It's as if I've known him all of my life, she thought.

CHAPTER 12

(The Producer)

"HEY, MAN, I'VE got the perfect person for you," said Derek.

"Who?" Jeremy asked.

"My wife can sing. She'll do it. She sings soprano."

Jeremy was a producer looking for someone to sing background on his gospel album. Jeremy was not only a famous producer, but he was also a doctor. His nickname was Dr. Benz.

"Can she really blow?"

"Man, I'm telling you she can blow, and she fine too," laughed Derek. Derek was always looking for a hustle, a way to make some money, so he figured if he got Trinity to do this album that would be more money, more fame, and more notoriety for him — plain and simple.

When Derek came home that night, he told Trinity about the producer and she was not happy about it at all. She wanted nothing to do with it or anything to do with Derek at this point. But Trinity was a devoted wife, so she agreed to meet him.

"Look, you better sing yo' butt off. We could make a lot of money off of this dude," Derek told Trinity.

So they went to meet him and as soon as Trinity saw him, she liked the way he looked. He was tall, built, a little gray and 55 years old. But she was a married woman. She shouldn't have been thinking about how good he looked anyway, but Derek kept egging it on. Trinity had to rehearse and audition non-stop.

Time passed and Trinity and Jeremy became really close. One night, Jeremy asked Trinity to go to dinner with him, and she figured it would be nothing more than a harmless dinner. After that date, they

(The Producer)

went on a second date to dinner and then to a hotel, and Jeremy blew her mind. He was so gentle with her. He treated her so tenderly. He had her all night and she enjoyed every bit of it. Not only did they record in the studio, he also took Trinity everywhere. It got to be so frequent that Trinity had to ask her girl Connie to be the middle man so Derek wouldn't become suspicious. Connie was always there for her when Trinity needed to be undercover with her shit.

"Hey, Connie, come and get me so I can hang out with Jeremy," Trinity would ask.

"No problem, but you know I'm gonna need a little extra paper," said Connie.

"Don't worry about it. I got you," said Trinity.

Money was not a problem for Trinity. Jeremy would give her anything she thought she wanted — money was never an object. Whatever Trinity needed for herself and for her kids, Jeremy was happy to accommodate. He spent thousands of dollars spent on expensive restaurants, beautiful clothes and anything else Trinity wanted, but it came at a price — adultery. Jeremy was married and so was Trinity, but it was more than that. They had begun to fall in love with one another. Jeremy was more than twenty years older than Trinity. He was fine, he was rich and he wanted her. He didn't care that she was married and had kids and she didn't care that he was married and in his fifties. But deep down, Trinity was lying to herself — she did care. She couldn't stand Derek, but she still believed in the sanctity of marriage. And as much as she loved being with Jeremy, she hated cheating on her husband.

During their affair, Jeremy's wife hired a private detective.

"Baby, I'm sorry, but we may have to slow it down or stop seeing each other altogether," Jeremy said. "My wife is crazy and I could stand to lose everything."

Trinity knew he wasn't going to leave his wife and give it all up, but she didn't care; she wanted him. What Trinity didn't tell Jeremy was that she was pregnant with his child. She never told him she was pregnant — not even after she had the miscarriage. Trinity knew losing the baby was the best thing because if Derek had any idea what was going on, he would have probably beat the baby out of her. Even though

"WHY"

they were together only seven months, Jeremy showed Trinity that she deserved more, and that she deserved to be treated with respect. No man had ever treated Trinity as well as Jeremy did. Once she got a taste of living better and feeling good about herself, it was hard for her to stay with Derek. Something was different about Trinity after she and Jeremy broke it off. She couldn't quite put her finger on it, but she was different. Stronger. She knew she wanted out, but she just didn't know how to do it. Fear can be crippling, especially when that's all you've known. All she knew how to do was survive in the fear. Besides, who was going to help her take care of her three kids until she finished school?

She hated to admit it, but she needed that son of a bitch. She needed him because she didn't know how to be without him. Derek was her first real love, so how could she abandon him and take her kids' father away from them? As usual, Trinity thought of everyone else except herself. The bruises on her body weren't enough to make her leave. The constant verbal abuse was just something else she figured she had to endure to keep her life and her children's lives comfortable. Talimah always knew when her mother fought with her dad. She could hear her mother crying in the middle of the night and wanted to run to her, but she was afraid. She was afraid her father would get mad at her.

"Is mommy crying again?" Tiffany asked. "Yeah, but don't be scared. Just go back to sleep," Talimah told her younger sister. Tiffany was Trinity's second oldest daughter and Talimah always looked after Tiffany. She protected her. When Trinity was out working and going to school, Talimah was in charge of looking after her siblings. She looked after Tiffany the same way Trinity used to look after Tasha. Derek didn't know it, but he was frightening his children. Their dad was supposed to make them feel protected and instead he was instilling fear. *Things have to change. I'm better than this,* thought Trinity. *There's got to be a way out for me.*

CHAPTER 13

(Having the Courage to Leave)

TRINITY WAS SO sick of it all, which is why she was on birth control. The last thing she wanted was to have another baby by Derek. She couldn't imagine how she would get out of this abusive situation, let alone bring another innocent child into it. She had three beautiful children by Derek, and that was enough, she thought. But little did she know, all of that was about to change.

Ever since Trinity was a little girl, she prayed, but now she couldn't even do that. Trinity hated herself and her life so much that she tried to commit suicide by ramming her car into a wall. Right before she was getting ready to hit the wall, her cell phone rang and it was her pastor, the secretary and the choir director. Little did they know, that is what Trinity needed to hear to stop her from an awful crash. She just wanted to feel love. After avoiding the car crash, she knew she had to stay strong for them for her children and herself. She knew if God didn't take her, then she had a purpose. Trinity knew that sometimes your children will give you the courage to change and become a better person, and this is why God blessed her with her miracle baby, Jordan. Jordan was conceived from Trinity and Derek even though Trinity was on birth control. Trinity had Jordan at the age of 24, four years after her and Derek's last child. Jordan was their miracle baby and he was also the strength that enabled Trinity to finally leave Derek. Derek would always say, "I'm going to leave you in this house with nothing," but it was Trinity who left him instead.

She had to do it quietly and without any suspicion or hesitancy. She didn't want Derek to beat her. Even though she was pregnant, Derek didn't care. He still abused her.

(Having the Courage to Leave)

"I hope you hemorrhage and die," was one of many hurtful things Derek would say to Trinity while she was pregnant with Jordan. On top of beating and spitting on her, Derek would oftentimes take Trinity's food and throw it at her so she couldn't eat.

Trinity finally sat down with her dad and mom and told them what was going on. She told them that she was leaving Derek and needed their help.

"What do you mean you're leaving Derek?" Trinity's mom said. "You better stay where you are. You've got those kids to think about."

"Shut up, Delores," yelled Trinity's father. "Didn't you hear this child say she was getting beat? Now shut up and let me handle this!" Trinity's father told her to let him know when she was ready and he would be there to help.

Trinity set it up so Derek had no idea that she was moving. He didn't know Trinity was leaving until her father and brother came to help her pack. Trinity moved just two weeks before little Jordan was born. She called him "J" for short. Jordan brought hope back into Trinity's life. With this newfound eagerness, she began her road to healing. But it didn't come right away.

Trinity moved out of the suburbs into a nice apartment, but she was still in love with Derek. She continuously made the mistake of trying to help Derek, but he was beyond help — at least from Trinity.

Throughout the years, Trinity never quit school. She managed to go to school part-time and graduate with a Bachelor's Degree.

"You a dumb ass chick. You will never amount to anything," was one of many things Derek used to say to Trinity. But Trinity got her degree while maintaining their household and children. When she moved and got her apartment, Trinity's father bought her a car because she needed it and he was so proud of her. Trinity's father knew Trinity was in hell, he just didn't know what to do and he hated himself for not doing anything. He figured maybe buying her a car would make up for all the times he wasn't there for his daughter. *I hope she knows how much I love her*, he thought.

Meanwhile, Derek knew he had lost control, and the only way Derek knew how to regain his control was to threaten Trinity with violence or taking their children. Trinity was doing just fine without Derek, even though she was living a double life. Trinity didn't know it, but Derek was jealous of her and he was pissed that Trinity managed to leave him, find an apartment with their kids, get a job and become self-sufficient. Unbeknownst to him, Trinity was also dancing to make ends meet. Dancing paid a lot of bills. She could easily come home with a thousand dollars a night. Even though Trinity only danced for eight short months, she was good and when she danced, she was fearless and the men loved it. As far back as Trinity could remember, she always led a double life, even when she was a little girl. She could've won an Oscar Award for all the lies she told and all the different people she had to become just to survive. *How had I gotten so far away from God*, Trinity thought. But old habits die hard and Trinity was used to having a man around. Derek knew how to push Trinity's buttons, so when Derek begged to come back to Trinity, she caved.

The first week went well, but that didn't last long. Derek was hardly ever home, probably somewhere gambling. And when he was home, he wouldn't help with the kids.

Why did I think this time would be any different? Ugh, I am such a fool, Trinity thought to herself. She was fed up. She had gotten a lot stronger and decided she wasn't taking his shit anymore.

"Derek, you gotta go," she told him one day.

"I ain't going no damn where. You gonna have to put me out," said Derek.

"Okay, if that's the way you want, then I'm calling the police," Trinity said.

Trinity didn't expect Derek to try and take Baby J with him. He snatched Little J up and ran towards the door. At the time, Little J was only 6 months old.

"Oh my God, Derek, put the baby down! Please put the baby down!" Trinity screamed. "I'm going to call the police! Put J down!" But Derek didn't listen, so Trinity called 911.

"Hello, could someone please come and get my husband? He's trying to kidnap our baby. We're not together. We're separated and he's

(Having the Courage to Leave)

drunk. I'm scared he's going to hurt our baby. Please send someone to help me!"

Trinity was hysterical, and the 911 operator was trying to calm her down enough to get the address. Derek was screaming in the background and Little J was crying.

"Hurry please!" Trinity yelled.

"After everything I've done for you, you're gonna call the police on me? I should come around this couch and beat yo ass!" Derek screamed.

"Derek, please put the baby down! I'll call the police and tell them not to come."

But it was too late. They could hear the police sirens coming down the street. Trinity ran towards the door, but Derek tried to block it. She still managed to get out.

"Sir, this is the police. Would you come out with the baby?"

"I ain't coming nowhere!" Derek shouted.

Trinity had also called the assistant pastor at their church, and he showed up pleading with Derek to let the baby go and come out. Finally, Derek listened and came out to be handcuffed and put in the squad car. After that Derek didn't bother Trinity anymore. Maybe because he was tired of being a jackass or maybe he had noticed that Trinity wasn't taking his shit anymore. Eventually, Derek moved to another state and Trinity began to heal.

After Derek and the police left, Trinity sat on the couch and reflected on her life with Derek. She sat there and just broke down crying and thinking of all the years of abuse, promiscuity and prostitution within her marriage. How would she explain any of it to her daughters? How can she tell anyone how miserable she was to have done the things she did? Who would understand? It wasn't just misery. It was years of being unhappy and being sheltered. *Who wants to be married and pregnant at seventeen?* Being with those men was a release and also just a temporary fix. Nothing could permanently fill Trinity's void but God. Because Trinity was so depressed, she started drinking and clubbing, and before she knew it, she was out in the streets just as much as she was in church. Trinity felt herself becoming this evil woman who wanted to hurt men. Trinity was always told that you can't serve

"WHY"

two masters, but she was serving the devil and God, and the devil was winning. She just wanted to numb the pain of constantly getting her ass beat. But she still prayed every night and would ask God, "Don't let me become this woman I feel I am becoming." She was going into a dark place and she didn't know how to stop it. All she knew was to pray and ask God to help her stop.

1 Timothy 6:10 says, "For the love of money is the root of all evil: which while some coveted after, they have erred from the faith, and pierced themselves through with many sorrows." Well, Trinity definitely pierced herself with many sorrows. She thought to be with different men would hurt Derek, but she was wrong. She did more harm to her soul than any harm she could have ever done to Derek. Every time she lay with a different man, she laid with his baggage. His sin transferred into her flesh. In the church, they call it soul ties. Sure she tried to convince herself that she needed the money, but truthfully, Trinity enjoyed being wild. She enjoyed controlling her own life because while she was married to Derek. He never let her control anything. Her prostitution had become a habit. Sometimes Trinity would meet a guy and if he only had twenty dollars, she would take it, just to have sex.

After their divorce, Trinity received $850.00 a month in child support. She also received food stamps, but sometimes she would convince herself that because she had four children, a car note, daycare and other bills, that the only way to make ends meet was to prostitute herself. She would often say, "I don't want to, but I need the money." There were times she would bring the men back to her home where her children lay their heads.

One night, she was at the club getting wasted, feeling good, looking good, and wearing her mink coat and fishnet stockings while her children were home alone. *What the hell was I thinking?* Thought Trinity. This particular night, she met up with her male friend at the club, and danced and drank all night. She got so drunk that she left the club and started walking down the street. Thank God for her friend. He took her home, undressed her while she vomited all over the place and put her to bed. He didn't try anything. Through the grace of God, no one

(Having the Courage to Leave)

ever harmed her. As Trinity sat on her couch, she knew she needed to do better. She knew this was no way to live. She knew something was wrong with her, but it would be years before she was completely whole. What she didn't know was that she would have to forgive herself and that would take time — years even. Sometimes God allows us to put ourselves in situations so we can eventually reflect on Him. If Trinity knew nothing else, she knew the Word of God — her grandmother and years of growing up in the church made sure of that.

Trinity knew that in order to thirst no more, she needed to turn her life over to God fully, just like the Samaritan woman in the bible. *(John 4:1-26)*. All of the men, all of the money and all of her sin would someday be used to teach others how to forgive themselves, how to believe in hope and how to live a life of righteousness.

No one is perfect, but we are made perfect in Christ! God's love is what Trinity needed. She asked God to pour out his love on her and he did just that. Jesus Christ's love brought her peace, security, and transformed her life. It began to heal her wounds from childhood to adulthood. She was receiving God's Love and it was amazing.

CHAPTER 14

(The Devil Tried to Trick Trinity)

SOMETIMES, BEFORE YOU get to what the Lord has for you, a lie will come in the form of the truth. That's what walked into Trinity's life after David. Three lies waiting to take what the Lord had for her. The Lord had a husband that would cherish Trinity and love her unconditionally, but the devil had his devices as well. The devil knows who is anointed and blessed beyond measure and he will come to steal, kill and destroy that very thing. Trinity's demons came in the form of three men who presented themselves as potential husbands:

-ANTHONY-

They had been best friends since college. They got along great. They had similar tastes and even laughed at the same things. Anthony was even the godfather to Derek and Trinity's son Jordan. Anthony is the one that picked Jordan's name. He had been a part of Trinity's family since forever. So when he heard Derek and Trinity were splitting up, he was shocked. Everybody thought they were the "it" couple. Time passed and they started hanging out more and eventually, they started dating. Trinity would soon be divorced from Derek, so she didn't think anything of it. *Why should I let Derek ruin my chances of potential happiness?* Trinity thought.

They partied all the time and when they did, Trinity was the center of attention.

"I want you looking A-1 all the time," Anthony used to tell Trinity. That meant he wanted her hair done, nails done, toes done all the time. Trinity had to be on point, no excuses — even if they were just chilling at the house, he wanted her looking "A-1."

(The Devil Tried to Trick Trinity)

"Why I gotta be A-1 all the time and you B-1?" Trinity would ask him.

"Because I said so. I want my woman looking good at all times."

Trinity was sick of his A-1 shit, but she didn't say anything. He bought the clothes and paid for everything, so why not?

"Damn, dog, you got a model on your arm. How you get a fly chick like that," one of Anthony's boys asked.

"Don't worry about it, lil nigga, just know she ain't yours," said Anthony.

When Trinity walked into the clubs, all eyes were on her. She looked good, she dressed nice and she always smelled good. Anthony loved that about her. She always smelled good and it turned him on. Anthony spoiled Trinity. He even bought her a truck. Trinity felt safe and protected with Anthony, not just because they went way back but also because Anthony was a police officer. Anthony told Trinity he believed she was the woman for him, but the kids didn't like him. Trinity's daughter Talimah would say, "Mama, we don't like him. Why are you with him? Something is not right about him."

Anthony didn't want anyone looking at Trinity or talking to her. He began to get very controlling. Something was a little off about him. Trinity found that out when they would be horsing around like they were play fighting. Anthony would punch her and put her in a police chokehold and then laugh it off, but he hurt Trinity. He bruised her.

"Ouch! Stop, Anthony, what are you doing?" Trinity asked him.

"Ah girl shut up you ain't hurt," he replied.

But Trinity was hurt, and not just physically. This was becoming all too familiar. It got worse when Trinity became pregnant with his baby. Anthony didn't want her to get an abortion, but Trinity just couldn't bring another child into this world — especially with someone like Anthony. She was heartbroken. She felt all alone and couldn't believe she killed a baby. She was glad Anthony went with her to the abortion, but she still felt like a murderer, and no amount of support was going to change that. They weren't together as a couple too much longer after that. They just hung out from time to time, but nothing serious. When Trinity met David, all of that stopped.

"WHY"

One night, she and Anthony ran into each other in the club. Trinity was buzzed and waiting on David to get there. She and Anthony started dancing and hung out for a minute until David got there. David remembered him. Since he was J's godfather, he had seen him around, and he knew Anthony and Trinity used to kick it. The next day, Trinity noticed her four-carat ring was missing. She called David and told him that she thought Anthony had taken it. She remembered feeling like he slipped it off of her finger, but she was buzzed so she wasn't sure.

The next day, David came back with her ring — Anthony's thieving ass did take it. To this day, Trinity doesn't know what David said to Anthony, but later on she got a call from him saying he was going to back up and stay away. She never saw Anthony again.

-MINISTER GEORGE-

By this time, Trinity was divorced from David and had been celibate and dedicated to her prayer life. She had begun to pray specifically for certain things she wanted in a husband. Then, in walks someone she already knew. David knew him too. His name was Minister George, and he would come and minister at their church from time to time. Minister George always liked Trinity. David knew it and he would tell Trinity that George liked her, but Trinity could care less. Minister George had a prophetic anointing and he always kept in contact with Trinity. He called Trinity one day and said he had been in prayer and that he was praying for her because he knew she had just gone through a divorce. Minister George asked Trinity out for lunch and since she and David were divorced, Trinity didn't see the harm in it.

Lunch and everything after that turned into a nightmare. They were talking and when it was time to go, out of the blue, Minister George asked Trinity to buy him a laptop. Most people who knew Trinity knew that she was well-off financially, but this fool had the nerve to ask a recently divorced woman with six children to buy him something.

"Excuse me. You want me to buy you what?" Trinity replied.

"You should buy me a laptop. You know you got it like that," said Minister George." Trinity couldn't believe that this man, better yet, this man of God was trying to hustle her. He even had the nerve to say, "God told me that you're my wife." Trinity was ready to go after that.

(The Devil Tried to Trick Trinity)

"Um, I'm ready to go," said Trinity.

"Yeah, okay, let's go," said Minister George. But before they could leave, he claimed he forgot his wallet and couldn't pay.

"What do you mean you forgot your wallet?"

"I forgot my wallet. Come on baby, you can pay. You know you got it."

This lunch date was going from bad to worse. Before it was all over with, Minister George asked Trinity to help him pay his rent, of which she replied no. Then, he had the nerve to try and kiss her and it was sloppy as hell.

"Stop kissing me," shouted Trinity. He had the nerve to think Trinity would have sex with him, and here she thought he was a man of God who didn't believe in sex before marriage. He was nothing but a fraud! Trinity was so pissed. This was not the man she prayed for.

-CRAIG-

Trinity and her family were raised in a very religious household, so when she met Craig, it was nice that they had that in common. Trinity was forever the romantic, ever since she was a little girl. *Maybe Craig might be the one I prayed for*, thought Trinity. She hadn't been with anyone sexually since David, and she was long overdue for some attention. But, the catastrophe named Minister George made Trinity not even want to try or believe that the Lord had someone for her. But Craig had all the attributes she prayed for. Along with having the same religious upbringing, he loved kids and he was easy on the eyes. Trinity liked a man who was buff, and that was Craig. Craig was playful, sarcastic and a lot of fun. He was Trinity's big ole teddy bear. He even told Trinity he didn't want to touch her sexually. He was willing to wait until she was ready.

They got along great and he even proposed to Trinity. He would say things like, "You're mine, your kids are mine and I deserve you." Trinity was so love-struck. She couldn't believe it was true. Could this man be the man that she prayed for?

Well, maybe he could've been the one for Trinity if he wasn't already married. Yes, married! Trinity was done. After that, she dedicated

"WHY"

her whole life to God, herself and her children. A year and a half later, she met Chris. Craig heard Trinity was getting married and had the nerve to call her right before her wedding and beg her to choose him! *Seriously?* She thought.

CHAPTER 15

(I Was His Personal Savior and Drug Mule)

"WHERE ARE YOU? Who are you with?"

"Look, quit asking me all of these damn questions and just bring me the money," David replied.

Trinity was so sick of this. *He's going to get me killed*, she thought. David, the man of God, her best friend, the father of her children, was a crackhead. What the hell kind of shit was this?! All of this happened only two weeks after Trinity and David had gotten married. *How could I have missed this?* Trinity thought. *How did I allow myself to get involved with this kind of shit?* In the beginning, Trinity thought he was just dealing dope, not smoking it. But David was a master at hiding the truth and after he and Trinity got married, he didn't care about hiding anything anymore. Everyone has secrets, but this was not a secret she thought would ever come out. After all, he was a Pastor—how could this be? *Here I go again with living a double life*, thought Trinity. No one could ever know what she had to help her husband with—no one. She wasn't used to this. Her first husband she could handle, but this man was something different.

Trinity couldn't understand what was going on at first because David showed no signs of this behavior when they were dating. Trinity knew David was no saint. She knew he had a hard childhood, and had spent time in and out of prison because he was in the drug game, but she thought that he was done with all of that. He wasn't a dumb dude. He had his Associates in criminal justice. He was a first-generation graduate.

"First Lady, Pastor David preached such an awesome word on today," said Brother Skaggs. "The Lord used him mightily."

(I Was His Personal Savior and Drug Mule)

Beaming with pride, Trinity looked at her husband. David was up there on that pulpit all sweaty, preaching the mighty word of God. He looked so powerful and authoritative that Trinity couldn't help but get a little turned on.

"Hey baby, take this towel so you can dry off. And here's a new shirt to put on," Trinity told David.

"Thank you, baby, what would I do without you?" David replied. She took good care of David. She was such a devoted wife and First Lady.

"You guys make such a nice couple and you're both so devoted to each other," said one of the brothers at the church. "Pastor, you truly show us men how to treat our wives."

"Thanks, man. That's my boo. I would do anything for her," said David. Brother Skaggs' wife later came up to Trinity and said she thought David was a good husband and father, and asked Trinity to pray for her husband. Trinity told her she would, and she and David and the kids got in the truck to go home. It had been such a beautiful day. The Lord proved himself mightily through David's preaching. Trinity was starting to forget that her husband, the Pastor of the church, was addicted. *I'm going to make him a nice dinner*, she thought as they drove home.

"Honey, are you doing anything today?" Trinity asked David.

"Naw babe, why?"

"Well, I just thought we could have a family movie night and I'll fix us a nice dinner." David loved doing things with the children. He was a good father and husband when he was at home. "Yeah that's cool, let's do it," he said.

When they got home, Trinity changed her clothes and David got the kids settled. Trinity started fixing her famous baked chicken, dressing and mac and cheese. David loved Trinity's cooking. When Trinity was almost done cooking, David said he was about to run to the store to get some good wine to go with dinner. "Hey, give me a kiss. I'll be right back," he said. Trinity didn't think anything of it until she saw that look in David's eye — she knew he was lying.

"No, that's okay babe. I'll go. I have to get something for myself anyway," said Trinity.

"WHY"

"Naw, just tell me what you want to get and I'll get it," David replied. She knew he wasn't coming back. Trinity began to cry and ask David to stay but that didn't do any good. It never did any good. Her tears and her pleading were never enough.

"C'mon, Boo, I'm coming back," David assured her. "Don't be scared and quit all that crying. I love you."

He kissed Trinity gently, hoping that would calm her down, but it didn't.

"Baby, please stay," Trinity continued pleading. "You've been so good lately and God really used you today. Please don't go."

"Baby, I ain't doing drugs no more. I'll be back. You don't have to worry."

Trinity didn't believe him, but she said okay and prayed for the best.

David kissed Trinity again, told her he loved her and left. Trinity waited all night looking out of the window, wondering if every car that went by was David's, but it wasn't.

"Mom, where is David? Trinity's daughter Tiffany asked. Trinity told her that David was at the church helping one of the members.

"But he missed dinner and we were supposed to watch movies," Tiffany said. Trinity hated lying to her children all the time.

"C'mon we can still watch movies," said Trinity.

Three days had gone by and there was no sign of David. Now Trinity was beginning to worry. Trinity did what she always did; prayed and cried out to the Lord asking Him why this was happening. *The ladies at the church are looking at my husband wanting what I have, but they just don't know how blessed they are; at least their husbands come home at night,* thought Trinity.

> Trinity turned the lights off and just as she was about to lay down, she heard something. "David, is that you?"
>
> "Yeah, it's me babe. I'm sorry I messed up again," said David.

Trinity was so disgusted with David. "Why do you keep letting the devil use you? He's laughing at you, David."

(I Was His Personal Savior and Drug Mule)

"Baby I know. You're right. Please don't do this now. We can talk about it tomorrow. Just rub my stomach. It hurts," said David. Trinity asked him did he have anything to eat while he was out there and he told her no.

"That's okay, baby, I'll fix you some tea and soup that'll make you feel better," Trinity told David.

David thanked Trinity and then he rolled over and cried, "Baby, I'm so sorry. I ain't shit for doing this to you and the kids. I'm so sorry. Please forgive me, baby."

"I know you're sorry," Trinity said. "It's okay. We can get through this together."

Trinity went into the kitchen and broke down crying.

"When is this going to stop? How much longer do I have to put up with this? Why God? Why are my prayers not being answered? Please save my husband. Please save my marriage!" Trinity cried.

Trinity arrived at the crack house at about midnight. Her kids were at the house asleep. Anything could've happened to them, but she was bringing David money so the drug dealers wouldn't beat him up and keep his phone. All this craziness because David owed them two hundred dollars! What would the congregation think if they knew their pastor and first lady were in these streets like this? Here they were the envy of the congregation, but in reality, they were close to being homeless.

Trinity was pregnant again with child number six and she couldn't even be excited about it. How could she be excited when they went from living in a lakefront mansion on a hill to a trailer park? David took Trinity and the kids from their apartment to a beautiful, four-bedroom, house on a hill just two weeks after they got married. The children even had their own master bedrooms with a bathroom. David had his faults, but damn it was nice living like a queen and Trinity enjoyed all the perks of being with a man like David.

This property gave Trinity hope. It was a land contract property that Trinity wanted to call her own someday. On the outside, their lives looked like a fairytale, but the truth was Trinity had to sneak and take money from their bank account to pay the mortgage. If she didn't, David would just smoke it up. He was always a mastermind when it

"WHY"

came to making money. At one time, his real estate company and his other businesses were booming. He had fifty properties and had even managed to stash away $500,000 for a rainy day, but the recession wiped out a lot of people. David would soon go through that $500,000 trying to keep his properties and pay for the mortgage on the mansion he and Trinity were living in.

"I can't believe I have to do this. This is all your fault," Trinity told David.

David just stood there looking stupid while Trinity tried to find something to wear. None of her clothes said, "I'm homeless and I need food," but that was almost near the truth. They had no food and now Trinity had to go down to the food bank just so they could eat. She tied up her hair and wore a scarf so she wouldn't be recognized. She was embarrassed and pissed. Trinity never figured that she would be getting food from the neighborhood food bank. Between the food stamps and the food bank, Trinity was able to feed her family. She even got assistance from organizations that helped clothe her children and supply them with backpacks and school supplies. They even gave her food for Thanksgiving and Christmas gifts for her and the children. Trinity felt a little awkward accepting gifts sometimes, especially when they were delivered to the house. She needed help, but she wondered what those people thought about her living in a big mansion.

Eventually, the money dried up and the inevitable happened — they would lose the house, the cars and the businesses. Thank God for David's mother because she let them use her truck for nearly six months. After that they were able to purchase a Dodge Neon for five hundred dollars; it was barely enough room for all of them to fit inside. Here they were, still living in a big house on the hill and driving a Dodge Neon. They were so embarrassed that they would pile into the car and drive away fast so that the neighbors wouldn't be able to see them. Now months into her pregnancy, Trinity had to find her family a place to live because David sure as shit wasn't going to. Thank God for Trinity's job. She worked in accounts receivable at a furniture store and she didn't make much, but it helped keep the family afloat.

I can't believe I'm out here looking for a place to lay my head, thought Trinity. She had been driving around all day looking for a place. When she

(I Was His Personal Savior and Drug Mule)

finally came across this trailer park, it was nice and it was on a lake. She always thought only poor white people lived in trailer parks but here she was, living like everybody else. With the little money Trinity had left, she was able to buy her trailer. No one could know — not even her family — especially her mom and dad. Trinity did confide in her brother Henry and David's mom, but no one could know that her husband had put her in this predicament. Trinity was David's wife and she was loyal to her husband, no matter what.

Totally embarrassed and feeling so alone, Trinity moved her family to the two-bedroom trailer. The boys didn't even have their own bedroom. They slept in the living room. Henry, Trinity's brother, had to help Trinity put a lot of her stuff into storage. The children were devastated. David kept making promises about these deals that were supposed to come through, but nothing ever came in except another bill. They would ride around and look at nice homes, but they never had enough money to move. And to make matters worse, David would leave to go on his binges, leaving Trinity without a vehicle.

"Where are you going, David? I need the car to take the kids to school," said Trinity.

"Look I'll be right back. I promise," said David. But David never came right back — especially if he had some money in his pocket or some way to get some dope on credit. Trinity was low-key happy when the neon broke down because at least he couldn't leave. But of course, David's mother would let him drive her car.

Trinity never did quit working and she eventually was able to buy a truck. That's one thing about Trinity — she never gave up and she always kept pressing ahead. Her children were depending on her and whether she knew it or not, so was her family. They always depended on her to be okay. But if they only knew Trinity wasn't okay for most of her life, she just faked being okay. When would she be able to rest? David certainly didn't give Trinity a chance to rest. She always was stressed out. If David was at home, he was sleeping off his binge and when he wasn't home, she still couldn't rest because she worried for his life.

During Trinity's life, she knew she had a relationship with God and she knew when God was talking to her. God always protected her,

"WHY"

even when it didn't feel like it. Trinity knew God was always around. One day the Lord revealed to Trinity that David was planning on getting his own place, away from her and the kids, so Trinity went on David's laptop to see if she could find any information and she saw his lease. The lease not only had his name on it, but Trinity's name was not on at all. *I know this mother scratcher is not trying to leave me here in this trailer with these kids*, thought Trinity. *After everything I've done for this nigga, he's going to leave me here in this damn trailer? How could he do me like this? What about his children?* Trinity wondered. After Trinity got out a good cry, she pulled herself together and went back into survival mode.

If this nigga is going to leave me, I'm not going to make it easy for him.

Trinity called the realtor and told him that she was David's wife and that they didn't want the property anymore. Even though Trinity tried to sabotage the deal, and after a heated argument, David still left her and the children in the trailer. Trinity and David's mother were close, which is why Trinity was shocked to find out that David's mother knew about his plans to move and didn't tell her. He couldn't even leave her like a man. He left her like a coward while Trinity was at the movies, and had the audacity to take their youngest son with him. Trinity had to drive to David's new house to get their son back. All of this drama was going on while she was still working and being in school part-time, working on her Master's degree. Trinity never stopped going to school. Even when her life was in shambles, she never gave up. Trinity didn't know it then, but she would tell her testimony to those that needed to believe that God always supplies us with a way out.

Of course David was on a binge when he was needed the most. It was during one of his binges that he missed his last son's birth. The only way David got notified about his son's birth was because Trinity tracked David's phone. Trinity was absolutely devastated. She was competing with the drugs and the drugs were winning.

Trinity had their baby without her husband. David was so hurt about missing his son's birth that he left for Miami two days after the baby was born. He told Trinity he owed his partner some money, so he was going to Miami to sell some dope so he could pay his partner back. Truth be told, David had smoked up his partner's share of the money and was in trouble. In the meantime, David sent drugs from Miami to Chicago for Trinity to sell. Trinity lied and told David's partner that David was in jail to buy David a little time so he could pay him back. But his partner never got paid back. When the feds began investigating, his partner just left. It was like he vanished into thin air. God worked that thing out because he was going to kill David's ass.

Six weeks after the birth of their son, Trinity got a call from David's cousin in Miami.

"Yo, Trinity, David down here going buck wild. You gotta come get him. He ain't listening to nobody."

Trinity, being the dutiful wife and after having just given birth, flies to Miami to try and rescue her husband — that was in February. She went back down to Miami in April, this time with the kids. She was sick of this rollercoaster ride. She was lying to everybody: her family, her congregation, herself. This wasn't God's best for her. This couldn't have been how God intended for her marriage to be.

Trinity began to pray about moving and eventually found a house. It was 2,000 square feet, two bedrooms, two bathrooms and a playscape out back for her children. She needed a deposit that she didn't have. As much as it pained her to pawn her wedding ring, she had to ask herself, "What am I holding on to it for?"

Trinity pawned her ring for two thousand dollars, but she still needed more money. The Lord said, "Ask your boss." Trinity had been working with this company for four years and had favor with her bosses. She asked for an advance of fifteen-hundred dollars. Trinity told her supervisor why she needed the money. Her supervisor was shocked because she always looked at them as a power couple.

"I'm sorry, Trinity, I never would've thought that you were going through all of this. You didn't show any signs of it here at work. Let me ask Mr. Fraiser and see what he says, but I think it should be okay. You're one of our best employees."

Not only did Trinity get her advance, but her bosses put her on a low payback plan of fifty dollars each check, and also gave her another position in the company. So now she had two jobs with the same company. When God is for you, no one can come against you and win!

"WHY"

Along with paying for her new house, she was stuck paying on the house David was living in before he left for Miami. Trinity did eventually move all of David's stuff into storage and let his house go. She couldn't continue to live like that and provide for herself and her children. Trinity even took David's son Rahim to live with her because his mother was unable to care for him. If Trinity only knew that Rahim would violate her loving kindness, she never would've let him in her house. She thought he could be trusted, but it turned out that Rahim was just as scarred as Trinity was when she was young. Just as he had been violated, he violated others to cope with his pain.

After living in Miami for four months, David came back to live with Trinity. She took him back against her better judgment, but she loved him she still wanted that fairytale of a happily ever after. David was so grateful to Trinity. He loved her beyond anything imaginable and he tried to do what was right, but it didn't last.

CHAPTER 16

(Dating the Old Fashioned Way)

TRINITY HAD NEVER been "courted" in the true sense of the word. If she met a guy and they hit it off, they would eventually sleep together then maybe get married. Or, Trinity would use them for money. With Deacon Chris, it was different. In the beginning, they talked on the phone and only saw each other at church. They were alone once and Deacon Chris hugged Trinity so tight but so delicate. It was their first hug and Trinity wanted to melt. Deacon Chris had a look in his eyes, and they both knew at that moment that they wanted each other. After that, Trinity's children would chaperone Trinity and Deacon Chris — they were never alone. Chris was always bringing Trinity cakes and banana bread. She loved banana bread. He brought her big boxes of lotions and other stuff from Bath and Body Works. He gave her beautiful antiques. He was such a romantic. Trinity prayed that he was the real deal. After a while, the children started to get used to going out with them and got upset when they couldn't go. They liked having the security of a two-parent household.

"Mom, can we hang out with Deacon Chris and go to work with him, please?" Trinity's son asked. Trinity knew that Deacon Chris owned his own landscaping business and was good with children. Her sons liked him, so she figured why not? At least they would be learning a craft and making money. Chris came from a two-parent household. His father taught him and his brothers the family business of landscaping, and Chris took the family business over eventually.

"Thank you for letting my boys come to work for you," Trinity told Deacon Chris.

(Dating the Old Fashioned Way)

"Not a problem, I could always use the extra help and its good for young boys to work. It keeps them out of trouble," Chris told Trinity.

Trinity came to the church to drop off the boys so they could go to work with Chris. When she walked through the door and took off her coat, Chris couldn't help but notice all those curves in that dress.

"Dang, I didn't know all that was in that dress," Chris told Trinity.

Time passed and Trinity and Chris became very close. He was proving to be a man of his word, not only to her but to her children as well. Trinity saw how attached her children were to Deacon Chris, and all she could say was, "Lord, I'm trusting in you." Deacon Chris's birthday was coming up and Trinity had the whole day planned. First, she took him to breakfast. After that, they went walking, then to lunch, then to a movie. At every destination, Trinity went into her trunk and pulled out a gift for Deacon Chris. He had never had anyone show him this type of love and affection. Trinity gave Deacon Chris, shoes, a watch, a couple of shirts and a bracelet. "Ah baby, you shouldn't have done all of this. I don't know what to say," said Deacon Chris. "This is beautiful and you are beautiful. Thank you, I will never forget this day!"

Deacon Chris was Trinity's prayer answered. Trinity believed in prayer and she knew the power of fervent prayer. As she began to heal and find herself, she began to pray differently and find value in herself. She hadn't known her worth before. Now Trinity prayed for what she believed God wanted for her life instead of what she wanted. Trinity learned that as she spent more time with God, she was not consumed with her flesh. God began to help her pray for not only what she needed, but also for what she wanted. It's a funny thing, but when we learn to sacrifice our flesh, God will give us the desires of our hearts.

"Honey, would you come and rub the back of my neck?" Trinity asked Chris.

"Yeah, sure baby, here I come."

Chris may have been a landscaper, but his hands were soft like fluffy cotton.

In his deep, Barry White voice, he asked Trinity, "How does that feel baby?"

"WHY"

"Oh, Chris, you know how to make me feel soooo good," said Trinity. Besides God, Chris had become her rock. When he touched her, she thought she would melt like butter. He caressed her skin so gentle and so lovingly. When he first kissed her, he fogged up her glasses. *Lawd this man makes me feel so good, I need to write a poem just about his hands,* thought Trinity. Falling in love was easy for them, but it was not well received by others in the beginning.

Chris took Trinity to meet his family in Indiana. They went to his brother's house for the Fourth of July. Chris has five brothers and four sisters. Only two of the sisters were there. Thank God, because they gave Trinity the third degree. Chris's older sister Julia did not like Trinity at all. She didn't even come to their wedding. She kept looking at Trinity up and down and asking her a bunch of questions like she was a child. When they got there, Chris just dropped her off with his sisters and left. *Ooh wait until I see his butt,* thought Trinity. The other sister was okay. She was his younger sister. After having Trinity meet his family, Chris was ready to meet Trinity's mother and father, but Trinity was a little apprehensive and didn't know what to expect. She figured she'd go and tell her parents about Chris alone.

"What the hell you mean you want us to meet a new friend of yours?" Trinity's father said. "I know what you mean by the word 'friend,' Trinity. No, no no, I don't wanna meet the nigga. Knowing you, you'll probably wind up marrying this guy."

Trinity's mother chimed in next. "Oh Lawd, not again. You know you can't pick good men, Trinity!

"Does he have a bank account? An IRA? What's his credit score? Do you know anything about his finances?" Trinity's father continued.

Just like Deacon Chris's family, Trinity's parents didn't welcome Deacon Chris with open arms either.

"No, Daddy, I don't know all of that stuff yet," Trinity replied. "I just didn't want to tell you because I didn't want you and Mom saying I was sneaking around like I did with Derek and David."

"You don't need another man. You need Jesus!" Trinity's mother screamed.

"But he's a good man. He's a man of God and I believe the Lord chose him for me," Trinity told her parents."

(Dating the Old Fashioned Way)

"Yeah, we've heard that before," they said.

Now was the task of Trinity telling David about Chris. *I don't know why I'm bothering to tell David anything; all he's going to do is be against it anyway*, thought Trinity. This was a phone call Trinity did not want to make and even though it was David's idea to leave and divorce Trinity, he didn't want her with anyone else. He still came around and was a father to their two boys, but he was also a father to Trinity's other four children by Derek. That was one good thing about him.

"Um, what you mean you're dating again and you believe it's serious?" David asked Trinity. "You know damn well you can't pick no good man, Trinity, and I don't want just anybody around our children."

"Why the hell are you screaming at me?" Trinity yelled into the phone. "It was your idea to get divorced in the first place! You said you wanted to live single and be alone! You think I'm just supposed to be by myself for the rest of my life?"

Trinity didn't let David get to her. She knew what she had with Chris. Chris was a gentle soul and Trinity knew that he cared deeply for her. Their courtship prepared them for any obstacles that would come their way.

CHAPTER 17

(Trinity's Broken Baby)

"NOOOOO!" TRINITY SCREAMED. "Don't take my baby, God!!! Please don't take my baby!!"

How does God take an innocent baby? "Why, Lord? Why would you take my child?"

Trinity just summed it up to God punishing her. *Maybe God is punishing me because I liked having sex. Maybe God was punishing me because I molested my brother's friends. Maybe because I committed adultery or maybe I'm just not good enough.* Trinity just couldn't understand why this was happening.

David didn't make it any better. He was trying to be supportive, but Trinity could tell that David secretly blamed her. *How could he blame me?* Trinity thought. *If it wasn't for all the stress that he caused me, maybe the baby would've survived!* She didn't know what to think, and then he had the nerve to say to her that he wanted more children. *This nigga must be crazy*, Trinity thought. *I'm NOT having any more children with him.*

Their poor little baby had always been sick even when he was in Trinity's womb. As Trinity lay in her hospital bed, she began to think back when she first got the news that something may be wrong with her baby. It had already been a bad morning. David was drunk and she knew he wasn't going to be able to go to the ultrasound with her. As much as she loved him, she was so tired of his mess. Trinity arrived at the ultrasound. She was about five months pregnant.

"Is something wrong?" Trinity asked the nurse. She thought it was odd that the nurse wouldn't let her see the screen. As the nurse turned the screen away from Trinity, she told her she was having a boy. "Is something wrong?" Trinity asked again. As the nurse turned to leave, she told Trinity, "I'll have the doctor come and speak with you."

Alarmed, Trinity called David to come to the doctor's office. Meanwhile, the doctor came in to talk with Trinity and he told her that her precious son had a disorder, and usually children with this particular disorder don't live past eight months. As the doctor was talking with Trinity, David finally arrived. *Why in God's name it took him an hour to get here is beyond me*, thought Trinity. She was too devastated to be upset with David right now. All she wanted to do was cry.

"Because his brain activity is low and it's a possibility your baby may have cleft feet and hands. Unfortunately, I do have to ask if you and your husband wish to terminate the baby," said the doctor.

"No, doctor, we're going to proceed with the pregnancy because we're saved and we don't believe in termination," David said. "That's for God to decide."

Trinity felt like she was in a movie and she was on the outside looking in. She couldn't believe what the doctor was saying. She had given birth six times and nothing was wrong with any of her other children. *So why this one? Why now?* Trinity thought.

If Trinity had nothing else, she had great faith. As the months passed, she never researched the severity of her baby's disorder. She believed in miracles and that was enough for her to go to a full-term pregnancy. The reason Trinity was even in the hospital having the baby was because she was at work when she noticed her baby hadn't moved in some time. Trinity being the workaholic that she was didn't want to leave work to go to the hospital. Plus she figured it was probably nothing to be alarmed about. But her supervisor thought otherwise and drove her to the emergency. David was on his way to school when Trinity called him to meet her at the hospital. While Trinity was getting her ultrasound, the nurse went to get the doctor. Trinity was still faithful, even though there were about four or five doctors standing in her hospital room, looking extremely worried.

"Trinity, your baby's blood flow and oxygen are going straight to you," they told her. "Your baby isn't getting any oxygen, so we're going to have to perform an emergency C-section."

"WHY"

While Trinity was getting prepped for surgery, her dad came. The C-section went well, but why wouldn't they let Trinity see her baby? David and Trinity's father asked the doctor not to let Trinity see the baby, she only saw the side of the baby's face as the nurses took him away to get cleaned up. His head was partially covered, he was crying and all she wanted to do was hold her precious baby.

"Let me see my baby," cried Trinity. "Why won't anybody let me see my baby?" Their beautiful baby boy was born with clef legs and feet and an enormous head. Trinity's baby boy would never go home; instead he was transported to another hospital. When Trinity went to see him, he had been rushed to Children's Hospital. He needed three blood transfusions and a tube inserted in him for him to breathe. David said the doctors were handling their baby rough.

"Honey, I swear it looked like he was looking at me and he wanted me to tell the doctors to stop hurting him," he said. "It broke my heart. I felt helpless."

He felt helpless because he *was* helpless. After Trinity had the baby, David was nowhere to be found. He just left. *How am I going to get home?* Trinity thought. Trinity had to call her Pastor and his wife just to get home from the hospital. She would've asked her parents, but she just couldn't tell them that she didn't know where her husband was. Trinity went to see her precious baby every day, sometimes twice a day. David's sister and his mom were also on standby in case Trinity needed transportation.

The phone rang. It was Trinity's mother.

"Hey Ma, what's up?" Yeah I can come, I'm on my way," said Trinity.

Trinity's mother worked at the hospital where little Benny was and she told Trinity to hurry up and get down there and that something was wrong with the baby. Delores had seen the baby and she knew he wasn't going to make it. Trinity called David right away so he could meet her and the kids at the hospital. She wished that she could depend on David, but she knew that was a crapshoot. Thank God for David's mother. She watched their kids, cooked, cleaned and was there for Trinity when she needed it most. She had been staying with Trinity

(Trinity's Broken Baby)

and was right by her side since she had the baby; because David sure as hell wasn't. He was M.I.A most of the time.

Trinity, her mother-in-law and the kids rushed to the hospital. Trinity was so scared. She knew something was wrong. She felt it. Trinity got to the hospital as quick as she could "Where is he, where is he, where is my baby, screamed Trinity?" The doctors were with him, they brought her up to speed on what was going on with her precious baby. With tears in her eyes, Trinity picked up her baby and held him close. She sat with him, prayed over him and for a while it seemed like he was doing okay. It seemed like his breathing was much better and he was going to make it but the doctors knew better.

"Would you like us to pull the plug?" asked the doctors. "NO", Trinity told them. She said that she would leave it up to God. As Trinity was rocking her precious baby, she noticed an angel standing on her right side (some would say the right hand of God came upon her), he was handsome and dressed in army fatigues, standing at attention. Trinity then heard the Lord say to her in her spirit, "I'm taking him." Trinity looked around in shock and she heard the Lord say it again. "I'm taking him,"

Trinity said to herself, "No, don't take my baby!" While Trinity was holding her fragile little baby, she noticed the machines began to beep. "His heart rate is dropping," yelled one of the nurses. Right there in Trinity's arms, little Benjamin died, he lived only four days. Everyone was crying, including the nurses. Trinity's children witnessed their baby brother pass away.

David and Trinity named him Benjamin Rafael. In Hebrew his name was Benyahmin. Little Benjamin was nicknamed "Ben and "Benny" by his brothers and sisters. The nurses even gave the children arts and crafts to help them cope with the loss of their brother. David's other son, Rahim, would even go on to letter his football jacket with the nickname he gave his little brother "Ben".

"Why did you take my brother?" Talimah sobbed. To this day, Trinity believes it was the hardest on her oldest daughter Talimah. Because the death of her little brother impacted her so much, Talimah would later go to college and study infantile diseases so she could help innocent babies.

"WHY"

Here Trinity was again, by herself feeling helpless. Benny was dead and David was nowhere to be found — probably out getting high. Trinity was so sick of David getting high. Any excuse to go on a binge and he was gone. David was constantly leaving her and the kids alone. She was sick of being a mistress to his drug abuse. It wasn't until the next day that David came home. *This nigga got the nerve to be depressed about Benny dying, but he wasn't here for me when it happened,* Trinity thought. *I wished he had never come home.* He had the nerve to blame her for Benny's death.

"You should've prayed harder. You didn't fast enough," he told Trinity.

"Me?!" Trinity yelled in response. "It was you who was taking all the drugs!!"

Benny's death devastated both Trinity and David. He left again, and this time he was gone on a three-day binge. As if that wasn't enough, Trinity never got a chance to grieve at the funeral because when they started taking the casket away, David just went off. He totally lost it. Trinity wound up consoling him, and her father was pissed.

"This was your time to grieve. Now you have to take care of him," her father said. "Look at him. He's up there acting like a damn fool. He took the spotlight off of you AND the baby!" He never liked David much anyway.

While everyone was inside at the repass, Trinity was in the car mourning. Her pain was so paralyzing that she didn't want to get out of the car. "Come on, Sissy," said Tasha. "We have to go."

"I just can't. Just leave me here please." Tasha went to go tell her father that Trinity wasn't getting out of the car.

"Trinity get out of that car," yelled Trinity's father. "You had all the time in the world to grieve when you were at the funeral now you want to grieve in the car?" "C'mon let's go, you shouldn't have let David take all the glory at the funeral!! You have people in there you gotta see and want to see you, so get up and dry your eyes and let's go."

Trinity had felt so alone all of her life. Now she was dealing with the death of a child alone; again. David was acting crazy and she had to be strong for everybody else. *When God is it ever going to be okay for me to break down?*

(Trinity's Broken Baby)

By now, Trinity and David had been married for five tumultuous years. They separated eight months after little Bennie passed. In the end, David violated Trinity for the last time. Most people would say she got fed up over something minor compared to all the hell he had sent her through but you never know someone's breaking point. Trinity's breaking point came by way of a 70-inch TV. After putting her life and David's mother's life in danger going to David's rescue, due to drugs, she took him back. After the many women outside of their marriage, she took him back. After abandoning her and the children to live somewhere else, she took him back. After having seen a text message he sent to his cousin bragging about finally being free and leaving her and the kids again to go live in his condo, she still had hope and loved him. But, now he had the nerve to steal their 70-inch TV out of their house for $300.00. It was then that Trinity realized that she couldn't save him.

David actually had the nerve to send her separation papers when he was the one causing all of the havoc. Before the ink had dried on their divorce papers, this nigga had the audacity to claim this Puerto Rican chick as the woman God sent him. David met her while he was doing community service for the church. They had programs that helped people get back on their feet from prison. She was fresh out of jail and crazy as hell. When the kids would go over to David's house, they would come back and report to Trinity that this lady was living with daddy. But David couldn't see how crazy she was because she was catering to his every need, even bathing him every night! He got a taste of her crazy after she moved in and started fighting and staying out all night. For once, David began to see how Trinity felt when he would stay out all night getting high and wouldn't call. Trinity was watching everything from the sidelines. She knew this was going to blow up in David's face — especially after the chick ran somebody over with her car. By the time all of that happened, Trinity and David's divorce was final. And little Miss. Sunshine was on her way back to jail. Good riddance.

Trinity couldn't believe their marriage was over. But truth be told, she was relieved because she may not have done it herself. He did them both a favor. They were so connected to each other physically, mentally and spiritually that if he had not asked for a separation, who knows how much longer they would have been on this merry go round?

To this day, Trinity and David still have a special bond. They are still good friends. He is a good father to their two boys and Trinity's other children, so much so that Derek gets jealous at the mention of David's name. The children go and visit and talk to David regularly. Whether David is still up to his old ways, no one knows but him and God. According to Trinity, David is back in school and getting his Bachelor's degree. He is sorrowful and apologetic that he treated Trinity the way he did. He wishes he had never let her go. She was the love of his life and for that, he will always be thankful.

In all adversity, there still lies a blessing.

CHAPTER 18

(The Wedding Day)

THEY DIDN'T KNOW it, but when they met, the voice of God would speak simultaneously to them, and in that instant, they would become one. They would fit perfectly together. Chris would sweep Trinity off of her feet. He was seasoned and very charming. Because of her past, Trinity didn't trust people — especially men — and she was always very cautious. She could be aggressive and controlling. She could be selfish and she could be the most giving person in the world. She liked that Chris was sure of himself, he was steady, and she felt she could rely on him.

For so many years, Trinity had longed for something and someone better. She knew that she needed to be respected by a man; a true man. She knew she was worth so much more but there were things she didn't know she needed, things that only Chris held in his hands. Chris made Trinity feel like no one could handle her and love her genuinely like him. Trinity never had a problem getting a man to put his hands on her, but the problem was, those hands of her past beat her down emotionally and physically. By the time Trinity truly submitted to God, she was empty, which was perfect for God because He could fill her emptiness with the things she needed; including a man designed for her. A man that would help fill her cup until it runneth over with love, joy and peace.

There was no playing games with Chris. With him, it was all or nothing. The need and ability to make Trinity feel safe, secure and truly adored was something only Chris could do because he was fashioned for Trinity by God. Before Trinity walked down the aisle, she started

(The Wedding Day)

looking in the mirror, reflecting on her life, thanking God for her true king. Chris was so much more than his past, Trinity thought. Chris was capable, self-assured and loyal, and now Trinity was about to marry this man God chose for her. They both went through their own hell to come into Christ and to come to each other.

"Look, I'm not coming to your wedding if it's on a Saturday. You know that's the Sabbath Trinity, so pick another day," said Trinity's mother. "Okay, mom, I'm trying to find another day that's not on Saturday or Sunday." Trinity was trying to set a date for her and Chris' wedding at the church and it was beginning to get a little difficult. Trinity and Chris wanted to get married in November before Thanksgiving so they could spend the holidays as a married couple with their families.

"Friday the 13th, are you serious? You're getting married on Friday the 13th? Do you know what day that is?" Trinity's mother said.

She was superstitious and believed getting married on Friday the 13th could only mean bad luck. "Yes, mom, I'm getting married on Friday the 13th. I don't believe in all that nonsense," said Trinity.

Besides, it was the only day that worked for Trinity and Chris. The wedding almost didn't happen. Trinity and Chris needed a certain amount of money to cover everything, from the hall, the caterer, the honeymoon, and clothes for the children among other things. It was Sunday and Trinity needed the deposit for everything by Thursday. She only had four days to raise ten thousand dollars. Trinity went into prayer and asked God if this was the man for her to marry, and to please show her a sign.

The Lord did show Trinity a sign. He had her walk into her boss's office and negotiate a new salary with a bonus. Trinity was good at her job, and her former employer wanted her back and was willing to pay her handsomely. After hearing that he could lose Trinity, her boss not only gave her the negotiated salary, he gave her a signing bonus as well and she got an advance so she was able to pay her deposit. The wedding was on! "Thank you Jesus!" Trinity shouted. The day of the wedding had arrived and Trinity was all set until her sister, Katina, told her that she absolutely could not wear the dress their mom had

"WHY"

made. Trinity's mother made Trinity a gold, champagne-colored dress for Trinity's big day.

"Look, after I finish your makeup, you have got to go find you another dress," said Katina.

Reluctantly, Trinity tried on the dress and Katina was right. She couldn't wear this dress. It made her look like she was an old woman; no sex-appeal whatsoever.

Where am I going to find a dress on the day of my wedding? Trinity thought. After her sister finished her makeup, Trinity began her search. She went to two or three different bouquets and time was ticking. She finally arrived at the place where she had favor. Surprisingly, Trinity found a dress the same color as the dress her mom made, but she didn't have enough money. The dress cost hundreds of dollars, but the owner told her that if she came up with two hundred more dollars, the dress was hers. Trinity called her sister and her sister paid the remainder. Now she had to hurry back, get dressed, finish her hair and get married. At this point, she was close to two hours late.

"She'll be here, Chris, don't worry."

People were coming up to Chris trying to reassure him that Trinity didn't get cold feet. Chris had gone from being nervous to just plain mad after he found out that she was okay. Even Apostle Love who was officiating began to get a little nervous.

"Hurry up, hurry up!" Trinity's family yelled as she rushed into the church. "Where were you? We were worried," said Trinity's family. I'm here now. That's all that matters," said Trinity.

"Hey, Trinity, it's almost time. Are you ready?"

"More than you'll ever know," Trinity replied.

She took one more look in the mirror and realized she didn't even look the same — she looked and felt complete. All the pain and misery she had gone through in her life had helped in making her whole. She had become a treasure not only for herself, but for her king. *Hallelujah*, thought Trinity. *Hallelujah!!!*

When the doors opened and Chris saw Trinity, his bride to be, he went from mad to all smiles. Nothing had prepared him for this moment. It's as if he had been waiting on Trinity all of his life. Their love for each other began before they even met and now they would spend

(The Wedding Day)

the rest of their lives together glorifying God. Chris looked at Trinity walking down the aisle, and thought about how beautiful she was and how she was all his!

Apostle Love was so happy to join these two. She knew they were fashioned for each other and that they would make each other very happy.

"Chris and Trinity, I understand that both of you have written your own vows," said Apostle. Chris and Trinity both looked at Apostle and nodded yes. "Well, Chris, whenever you're ready, you can proceed. Chris had written his vows and now he was thinking, *did I write enough?* He just wanted everything to be perfect and he wanted Trinity to know how much he loved her.

CHRIS'S VOWS

Trinity, when I first met you I knew you were the one because God told me you were. With every breath I take, I feel relieved in knowing that God has returned my rib back to me, its rightful owner. And with that, I now can breathe again properly, officially knowing that God has blessed me not only with the woman of my dreams, but with the woman of my prayers. I thank you for allowing me to be your friend as well as your husband. I am grateful that you chose me to be your lifelong commitment.

With tears streaming down Trinity's face, she wondered if she could get through her vows. She was just in awe of how God had manifested everything.

"Okay, Trinity, you can do this," said Apostle Love. *Hold it together a little while longer*, Trinity told herself.

"Trinity, it's time for your vows."

TRINITY'S VOWS

My love, my treasure, my King, my gift from God. You chose me out of the belly of the Holy Spirit, which sealed my life with you. I am amazed at how the Lord put us together, so finely fitted for each other. You are my inspiration to do better, be better and love harder. I am your queen and you will forever be my King. I cannot express the joy you bring to my life, my heart and my

"WHY"

overall being. My time with you cannot be measured; it's infinite, just like Christ. We are boldly inheriting each other's past and through God's will, we're organizing our future. I am happy to be your bride, your partner and your lover. Thank you for choosing and loving me.

With delight in her voice, Apostle Love proudly said, "I now pronounce you husband and wife. Chris, you may kiss your new bride!"

"Why are you nervous? I'll take good care of you," Chris told Trinity.

"I ain't nervous. You just got that look in your eyes like you're getting ready to tear me up," laughed Trinity.

Trinity and Chris had been waiting until their wedding night to make love. They both wanted something to look forward to and Trinity was nervous as all get out. She had six children and had been married twice before, but it was something about this man, she thought. She began daydreaming about those mornings back when they were courting. Chris would give her massages while they would share great conversations. His hands were healing like a real masseuse, and he made Trinity melt every time he touched her.

"Honey, put your hands right here." Trinity took Chris's hands and put them on her neck. She was so tense and tired of everything she and the kids were going through with David. The children were transitioning and going through their own hell because of the divorce and it all seemed to rest in Trinity's neck and back. "Baby your back and neck feel like a bag of rocks. It's not good for you to be this stressed. I'm going to have to massage you every other day. Come here and let these anointed hands take care of that," Chris joked.

Trinity loved it when he touched her. She was so used to holding things inside, but not around Chris. He was her Doctor Feel-Good.

"Hey, baby, where your head at? Whatcha thinking about? This is our wedding night and you've disappeared on me." Chris said.

"No, honey, I'm right here. I was thinking about when we first started courting and how you used to massage my neck and how soft your hands were. I couldn't believe how soft they were for you to be a landscaper," joked Trinity.

(The Wedding Day)

"What you mean *was* soft? Baby, my hands still make you melt," Chris laughed.

And at that moment, he touched Trinity like she had never been touched. It felt like electricity was going through her whole body and pins were sticking her from her fingers to her toes. His touch was so pure and loving. He was such a gentleman, but Trinity knew he couldn't wait to tear her up. The way Chris caressed and kissed her ever so gently made Trinity feel like she was in heaven. She had never felt like this with any other man before.

Lord, if I'm dreaming please don't wake me up, thought Trinity. *This man is too good to be true. He truly is sent from heaven.*

"Turn over, baby," Chris whispered in Trinity's ear. The way he moaned and nibbled on Trinity's ears was as if he had never had a woman before. It made Trinity release herself fully to him, something she had not been accustomed to doing with any other man. This was more than sex. It was more than lust. It was more than anything she had ever experienced and he hadn't even entered her yet. He moved his hands up and down her body, as if he was trying to remember what she looked like with his fingers. Trinity quivered underneath his touch. She was ready to give him all of her. She thought this night would never come. This was her knight in shining armor that she used to daydream about when she was a little girl.

He's real, he's here and he's all mine, thought Trinity. It felt so good that Trinity began to cry.

"What's wrong, baby?"

"Nothing's wrong. It just feels so good," Trinity replied. "I don't want you to stop."

"I'm just getting started," said Chris. "We're gonna be here all night. You ain't going nowhere and I ain't going nowhere. We're in this for the long haul.

CHAPTER 19

(Elder Mitchell's Story is Still Being Written)

"Elder Mitchell, I just wanted to say that your sermon blessed me tonight. It was as if you were talking directly to me. My faith has been tested lately, but listening to you made me want to continue to believe the word of God," said a young lady.

"Thank you," said Elder Mitchell. "That's why I preach the word of God, because others need to know that He is sovereign."

"Excuse me, Elder Mitchell," yelled a woman from across the room. "Thank you so much for waiting...whew, let me catch my breath. I was so scared I wouldn't be able to talk with you before you left."

"How can I help you?" Elder Mitchell asked.

The lady was a loyal follower of Elder Mitchell, but she never had a chance to meet her. "Well, first, my name is Sophia and I have wanted to speak with you for such a long time, but I never could catch you. Thank you for waiting to speak with me," said the woman.

That happened a lot. Elder Mitchell was in demand. People came from all over the world to hear her speak. She spoke of things others were afraid to talk about, and things she used to be afraid to talk about. Most of her days were filled with prayer and waiting on the Lord to guide her steps. She had been blessed with a husband who supported her and a church home who allowed her to preach so she could hone her gift. She began speaking and giving teachings under the guidance of her Apostle. There, she saw her grandmother's prayers being answered. Elder Mitchell's gift was that of a prayer warrior and a great intercessor chosen by God to intercede on behalf of others. She had been a prayer warrior since she was a little girl, and no matter the

(Elder Mitchell's Story is Still Being Written)

struggles she went through in life, she knew how powerful the Lord was. Apostle Love welcomed Elder Mitchell and her children into her church family. Eventually, Elder Mitchell would begin to teach a few bible studies and many sermons. She did a women's conference titled, "There is a Queen in You" and another teaching titled, "No Matter What You Go Thru Give God Praise." She believed all women were queens, and she founded young girls and women's empowerment programs to teach and promote just that. When she ministers to women and young girls, she is noted in saying, **"There is a queen in all of us. We just haven't been shown how to access it."** Elder Mitchell's sermons of **"Royalty Within Us"** and belonging to a royal kingdom have impacted millions of women globally. Elder Mitchell also began to speak outside the church walls. She spoke for corporations where she talked about believing in yourself and having faith in your abilities to achieve what was thought to be impossible. Apostle Love also asked Elder Mitchell if she would tell her testimony.

"Apostle, I don't know what to say. Thank you for asking me, but my past is very colorful and I don't know how people will receive it," said Elder Mitchell.

"This is why I'm asking you to do it, daughter," said Apostle. "The saints need to know that no matter where you come from or the things you've done, God always has a plan for your life." That was the hardest sermon that Elder Mitchell had to preach.

After preaching that one sermon, many others followed her and she has never looked back. She is a true example of how the Lord can bless you and save your life even in your sin. Today, her life is nothing short of a miracle. Her testimony has not only been for other people to get healed, but it has been a blessing for her own family — especially her daughters. However, at the age of sixteen, Elder Mitchell's true passion wasn't ministry. It was becoming a forensic pathologist. She was inspired to go into this field of study after her grandmother died. Her grandmother was her only strong black female role model. When she died, all Elder Mitchell wanted to do was help others, and she figured determining the cause of a loved one's death would be of good service. But that was not the Lord's will for her life.

"WHY"

Elder Mitchell has become a strong woman in the Lord and it has not been easy. The Lord wanted her to share her story by writing a book.

"Lord, what do you want me to say? Where would I begin? Elder Mitchell asked the Lord. "What would my mother and father say? They wouldn't want me to tell our family business. How can I talk about what happened to me as a child? *Speaking about it at church or at a conference is a lot different than having it in book form*," thought Elder Mitchell. She had traveled the world and saw so much abuse women endured. She knew she was obligated to tell her story.

Some abuse we can't help and some of our sin is forced upon us when we are children due to our stolen innocence. Maybe I'll start my book there, thought Elder Mitchell.

"I think I'll call my character Trinity."

CHAPTER 20
(WHY)

SOMETIMES AS WE go through the different trials in our lives, we ask the question why? Trinity asked these questions time and time again, but she never got her answer until the Lord trusted that she could handle the answers. Maybe in your life you've asked some of these questions. If you have asked these questions and still have not gotten an answer, be patient, continue to do the Lord's work and when He trusts that you're ready, He'll give you the answers.

Here were a few

- Why does the Lord allow certain things to happen?
- Why is my heart always being broken?
- Why is my strength only in my faith?
- Why does my life look blurry before my blessings?
- Why does my pain have to be used for educational purposes?
- Why does my pain have several names?
- Why is it never enough to just do what I want to do?
- Why did my daughter experience some of my past pains?
- Why does a man hit with his fists and bite with evil words, only to chew on my pain and spit in my face?
- Why does the truth come in the form of a lie sometimes?
- Why choose me to suffer?
- Why am I still afraid?
- Why was my child born with a deformity?
- Why do I let men treat me this way?

(WHY)

- Why am I not good enough?
- Why do I have low self-esteem?
- Why do I attract these types of men?
- Why do I have to keep fighting?
- Why should I believe God?

These were questions Trinity asked herself for years and sometimes, depending on what she may have been going through that day, she still may ask the same questions. Some of you may have or are asking yourself these very same questions, and that's okay. It's okay to be unsure, it's okay to be afraid and it's normal to question God. However, in those moments, try to remember that the Lord will give us no more than we can bear. We must believe in ourselves and we must believe **WE ARE WORTHY!**

TRINITY'S LIGHT-BULB MOMENT:

Trinity's light-bulb moment and the answers to all of her "whys" was the moment when she realized that she was **WORTHY!** The reason she allowed men to treat her the way they did was because she didn't know her value or her worth. She did realize God allowed some of those things to happen to teach her who she was, and Whose she was! She was a child of God and He had to teach her to have faith, gain courage, believe she was a treasure, and learn to appreciate who she was. God taught her not to judge others through her brokenness and taught her patience through longsuffering.

Trinity understood that her testimony was not only for herself but for others. Her prayer is that her testimony will be a blessing to others, but more importantly to show how sovereign God is!

"He will not forsake us if we diligently seek Him!"

Deuteronomy 31:8 New King James Version (NKJV)
⁸ **And the LORD, He is** the One who goes before you. He will be with you, He will not leave you nor forsake you; do not fear nor be dismayed."

"WHY"

Her whys turned into why not I? As tragic as it was to lose a child, God gave us His only son. We all go through sufferings and Trinity wouldn't wish her pain and suffering on anyone. It's not the war that we all rage against, it's the reasoning behind it.

"Once we learn to walk in total faith and self-love, we will not allow people to treat us any kind of way and we will better understand our purpose in life," says Trinity.

Trinity's life is still unfolding and yes, she will continue to go through pain, experience joy, have setbacks and at times question God, but today she walks in the wholeness of knowing who she is!

She is a woman with purpose, self-worth and self-esteem that is earned every day!

"To the readers, live your life out loud, experience life with no regret but only the regret of allowing others to misuse and abuse you."

YOU ARE WORTHY!

Love,

Trinity

ABOUT THE AUTHOR

Elder Lakina Fulks is a wife, mother, entrepreneur, and now she's added author to her ever-growing bio. She is a successful businesswoman who believes in giving back, which is why she wrote this powerful book. She wanted this book to be a navigational tool that tells abused women and young girls that they don't have to take it anymore! Along with running her day-to-day business as a REALTOR® and Licensed Broker, she is the founder of **The Treasure Within,** a girl's empowerment program and the vice-president of **The Lost and Found Christian Association.** The Association's mission is to provide battered and sexually abused women and their children with a rehabilitation process that provides continuum care and empowerment while partnering with organizations and businesses who share the same vision. Elder Fulks is also a domestic abuse survivor, who in spite of everything carries herself with grace and dignity. **"WHY"** is her first book and she authored it with much trepidation. She knew that it would receive criticism and ruffle some feathers, but she did what the Lord commanded her to do. In the end, **"WHY'** has become an inspiration for many and hopefully the first of many books to come!

www.ingramcontent.com/pod-product-compliance
Lightning Source LLC
Chambersburg PA
CBHW050601300426
44112CB00013B/2015